The *Hofner* Guitar – A History

by

Gordon Giltrap

&

Neville Marten

Hal Leonard Books
An Imprint of Hal Leonard Corporation
New York

Contents

Photo credits: guitar photos, pp. 13–17, © 2009 Alan Cramp, Antonio Ongarello, Steve Russell, Graham Shaw; guitar and archival photos, pp. 13–20, © Karl Höfner GmbH & Co. KG; all other photos (first edition) by Neil Cope and James Cumpsty

Second edition published in 2009 by Hal Leonard Books (an imprint of Hal Leonard Corporation), www.halleonard.com. First edition published in 1993 by International Music Publications Limited.

Book design by Panda Press, England; Cover design by Adam Fulrath

Library of Congress Cataloging-in-Publication Data is available upon request.
ISBN 978-1-4234-6274-3

Printed in the United States of America

Gordon Giltrap

As far back as I can remember I have had a fascination for Höfner guitars. For me they conjure up part of the spirit of late 50's and early 60's Britain, a time just a few years after the war when austerity was still to the fore in the UK. How ironic that a small German company opened the door to affordable instruments ranging from beginners' models to the beautiful Committee and the flagship archtop, the Golden Höfner.

The early Committees' tables were made from carved pine and offered superbly designed flowing lines, stunning inlays, and that fishtail headstock. Some were just straightforward acoustic models while others sported distinctive single coil, slim-lined pickups, later to be replaced by more refined and powerful versions. These guitars were regarded as so beautiful that they even fitted a transparent pickguard.

In the UK artists like Tommy Steel and session guitarist Bert Weedon were seen playing these German works of art. The timbers used were the best you could get at the time, superb bird's eye maple for the back and sides and a mixture of ebony and rosewood for the fingerboard and floating bridge. Later on Paul McCartney would bring his famous violin bass to the world stage.

Most of the young players I knew yearned for a U.S. made guitar, but a Höfner was an attractive alternative—and affordable if you went for one of the solid-bodied varieties like the Galaxy or Colorama. For a kid like me from the back streets of southeast London's Deptford, though, this was completely out of the question, so I just had to be content to gaze longingly and lovingly in the window of my local guitar shop, dreaming that one day I might be able to save up the 90 or so guineas to buy one. A fortune!

In the meantime my father stood as guarantor for a nice little Höfner Verithin complete with Bigsby tremolo arm and fitted case. I didn't really play that guitar for very long, as I caught the acoustic bug in the 60's with the advent of Donovan here in the UK, the great Dylan from across the pond, and later the British school of guitarist songwriters spearheaded by Bert Jansch, John Renbourn, and Davey Graham. Of course a semi-acoustic with a Bigsby was no use whatsoever for this kind of music, so it went the way of many of those early instruments in a series of part exchanges for more desirable and playable acoustic guitars.

I now wish I had been able to afford to hang on to that first Höfner, but I still carry the memory of it with me, and from time to time get misty eyed when I see a mint-condition Committee from that period for sale somewhere. I still regard them as the most beautiful guitars ever made.

My first dalliance with a decent electric guitar was when my schoolmate lent me his blonde Höfner Club 50. At the time we lived in a Northumberland seaside village, and he and I would sit at the open upstairs window of his mother's social club on a Saturday morning, him playing the guitar through a Watkins amp and the two of us harmonizing a song, usually the Beatles'Ticket to Ride.' My voice hadn't broken so I took Paul's top line.

But one weekend he went away and lent me his guitar—I usually only got to look at it—and I remember going home and actually making believe it was mine. The neck was huge then for my little hands, but the cambered fingerboard and low strings made it much easier to play than my flat-necked Rosetti Lucky 7 with its egg-slicer action. I loved the black plastic pickups, the 'Höfner' transfer on the guitar's front, and the big, warm tone that emanated from it.

Neville
Marten

However, it wasn't long before another friend got a red Stratocaster—60gns, second-hand from Windows music store in Newcastle—and my head was turned. I later fell in love with Gibsons, too, but always thought a Les Paul was hollow, like a Club 50, until I was rudely awakened on eventually picking one up.

I recently replaced my Club. This one's an early Club 60, and it's a stunner. It took me 25 years to get it, and I don't intend to part with it in a hurry …

Christian Benker

Hofner's President

Karl Hofner began his musical instrument company in 1887, in Schonbach, in the eastern part of Germany. At that time, Hofner specialised in the construction of top quality violins, cellos and basses. Karl had two sons,Josef and Walter, both of whom came to work within the Company, Josef handling the running of the business, while Walter was more involved with production (he was also responsible for the development of the 'Beatle' bass). The two sons inherited the Company when Karl Hofner retired; this was shortly after the end of WWI and the Company's subsequent relocation to Bubenreuth, in what was to become West Germany.

When Josef, the older of the brothers, retired, Walter assumed control of the business, assisted by his daughter Gehilda, who shared both the management and the ownership of the Company.

Christian Benker married Gehilda in 1957, joining the management team and eventually taking control when Walter Hofner died, in 1982. Today the Benkers run Hofner, along with their own daughter Bergitt and her husband, Thomas Lichthardt; the Lichthardts representing the fourth generation of the Hofner dynasty.

The following interview was conducted with Dr Benker in Bubenreuth during the summer of 1992.

There was a rumour that some of the fine veneers used in the crafting of Hofner guitars came from Pullman train cars that were dismantled after the War. Is there any truth in this?

This is nonsense. We have always used timber, cut ourselves or bought, which was then seasoned and kilned and then made into guitars.

What timbers are used in the construction of a cross section of Hofner guitars?

The tops are made of spruce from Germany, mainly from the Bavarian Forest, near the frontier with Czechoslovakia. The backs are made of maple; the birdseye maple comes from Germany or other parts of Europe. The fingerboards are made of Indian rosewood, or ebony which comes from both India and Africa

Our plant at Hagenau (about 5 miles from the main factory at Bubenreuth) is the centre of wood preparation. Here the wood for the necks of the guitars is kiln dried after it has been naturally seasoned.

Are any of the old luthiers still working for the Company? In particular those who built the Golden Hofners and Committees?

Our luthiers for the master models were trained by the original luthiers. Unfortunately the old luthiers are now all dead.

Are there any pristine examples of Hofners in any museums anywhere, or are there old parts left in the factory which could be made into new instruments?

There are no examples in museums, but there are bound to be some collectors' items in private hands. We have a few unsold models from the early days in our own collection, and a 'Hofner Club' has been established in America. There may be similar clubs in Japan, because of the continuing popularity of the violin bass in Beatles fan club circles there. Alas, most of the older instruments have long gone. We have some old unfinished parts at the factory, but not all that's necessary for the completion of guitars. We still have some Golden Hofner necks stored away for sentimental value; the Golden Hofner remains one of the stars, because it is unique in its fancy neck and headstock work.

If you were to make a Golden Hofner today, what would you estimate to be the cost, using the original processes?

About £2,500.

To what extent did demand necessitate the introduction of mass production techniques, as opposed to Hofner's traditional hand methods?

The demand for our Jazz guitars has never been so high as to warrant a radical change in production processes. They have always been individually hand-made, as have the Archtop models and the Beatle basses.

The closest thing we have to production line operation is for the cheaper models, and these are produced in batches of only fifty or so on a so-called 'serial' basis. Specialised machinery exists in the plant for repeated standardised patterning, carving, planing and drilling operations on these particular batches.

Hofner's main endorsee has been, of course, Paul McCartney. Is there any information on him from the past, regarding the Company's relationship with him? Is there anything ongoing with him?

Hofner has never had any direct contact with Paul McCartney. In the early days, however, a Mr.Davis, who acted as a rep for Hofner in the U.K during the sixties, approached Brian Epstein on one or two minor technical points. I hope to have the opportunity to meet Paul one day, but there is nothing scheduled at the moment.

Are you still concentrating your efforts on providing instruments for top professional musicians?

Yes. We are an old family firm, with traditions to keep alive, resulting from our original involvement with violin making, when the firm produced high quality instruments for a very small number of customers.

What has been the state of production since the Beatle bass came out? Have there been any noticeable increases or falls in demand?

Since the War there have been a number of phases of guitar production worldwide, coinciding, naturally enough, with the rise and fall of particular trends in music. In the fifties, for example, the Jazz guitars and Archtops were constantly in demand, to be replaced in the sixties by more solid-bodied models. During this period there was a European/American struggle for market domination of the electric guitar.

How did Hofner cope with the huge influx of Japanese guitars which flooded its main markets from the sixties on?

Of course Hofner moved with the times and produced some solid-bodied rock guitar models, especially throughout the mid to late sixties. In the seventies the Japanese entered the solid-body market in a big way, and Hofner simply could not compete with these new models in terms of price, although the quality was broadly similar, if not slightly better than the Japanese.

So in the end we decided to concentrate on our traditional selling points, as trend after trend came and jazz became popular again. The Hofner Jazz and Archtop guitars were continued, and we also opened a new line of classical models.

Hofner stayed with their special models and left the Japanese firms to concentrate on the mass produced 'consumer' models. Hofner is the leading producer of classical high quality guitars in Europe, beating even Spanish producers in terms of sales.

What does the future hold for a family firm like Hofner? Will you keep to the tried and trusted formulas, or respond to new developments in music and technology?

Hofner has a company tradition that goes back over 100 years, and over 300 years as part of the accumulated tradition of fine instrument-making in our part of the world. We have always been interested and concerned about making instruments which, after purchase, will last forever. Every aspect of the construction of a Hofner instrument, therefore, is designed with this in mind. The toughest, most flexible, purest and tonally successful woods have always been used - European spruce at first, followed by cedar when the spruce began to be depleted. As a consequence, our models have been shown to be climate resistant, durable under very testing conditions, and still play perfectly even after years of use.

Of course, when new treatments, techniques or raw materials are available in the future, we will exploit them in our production, to keep the Hofner tradition of quality going. All our classical guitars - even those in our 'consumer range', which are our cheapest guitars, conform to these ideals. We choose to go up-market and sell at a higher price range, because cheaper materials and techniques from some competitors simply do not provide good instruments.

But we are not trendsetters in technology. We follow trends in updating the designs of, for example, machineheads and pickups. Of course our solid-bodied models have not been on the scene so long, so it has been easier for us to update and improve these from scratch.

But Hofner's Archtop and Jazz models have a long and unbroken lineage, and a reputation built on the basis of their purity and our unwillingness to deviate from a proven formula. Like I say, a Hofner is a guitar built for life.

Introduction

This book does not pretend to offer the whole Hofner story. It does not detail every instrument manufactured, or list each key worker employed by this great company from its beginnings in Schonbach, in the late 19th century, up until its present location in Bubenreuth, in what used to be called W.Germany.

Prior to 1958, Hofner guitars were not evident in the UK, other than those examples imported by groups returning from the Hamburg nightclubs, or by guitar-playing servicemen bringing home souvenirs of their stints in Germany. The reason for this dearth was that, although Hofner had been producing guitars from their new factory at Bubenreuth since the beginning of 1949, the instruments were not officially imported into the UK until Selmer of London took on the distributorship around 1958. But the guitars built for Selmer were specific to the UK and therefore different from those models supplied to the domestic German market. It was therefore deemed reasonable that a book aimed primarily at British readers should deal with the best known instruments imported by Selmer, and to which British enthusiasts could relate. But our horizons are narrower even than that…

Towards the end of the sixties, Hofner became embroiled, as did so many guitar companies around the globe, in copying the designs of the big American firms, primarily Gibson and Fender. However, unlike the Japanese factories, Hofner did not produce exact replicas of Les Pauls, ES335s, Stratocasters, Telecasters and so on (in retrospect, perhaps this was a mistake), yet the company still sacrificed much of its personality in openly emulating the market leaders. And when, after a few years, they could no longer compete against the Far East, Hofner gave up competing altogether and went back to building mainly archtops, classical guitars and Beatle basses for the Continental European market.

This book therefore highlights mainly those 'original' instruments imported into Britain during Hofner's 'golden period' between the late fifties and early seventies – the Clubs, the Congress, Senator, President, Committee, Golden Hofner, Verithin, Beatle bass and so on; guitars which formed only a part of Hofner's total production but which were among its most prestigious.

So, a narrow model line and a relatively short period of Hofner's history. But for British music this was an exciting and formative decade or so, and the range of guitars imported from Germany by Selmer of London was so influential as to be dubbed, by more than one commentator, 'The guitars which shaped the sound of British rock'n'roll'.

The section written by guitar 'guru' Paul Day should help clarify the date of manufacture of Hofner guitars, but it should be understood from the outset that accuracy regarding anything to do with Hofner guitars is almost impossible to guarantee. The guitars' tops did receive date stamps on their undersides, but this is quite difficult to locate and, even then, only tells part of the story. In reality, if an instrument bears several hallmarks of a certain era – pickups, control layout etc. – that's normally enough to guarantee its integrity.

We have used Hofner's own data for assembling the information in this book, and that is often scant and/or contradictory. So we trust mistakes or omissions will be excused. In any case, rather than a guitar-spotters' directory, this is a book for those who recall Hofner guitars with affection, or perhaps who simply mourn the loss of a particularly charming era in British popular music.

The artists who kindly agreed to be interviewed for this book recall the excitement of those 'Hofner Times' and highlight the influence of this manufacturer over the development of British popular music.

G.G./N.M. 1993

About the photography

The colour photographs of Gordon Giltrap's Hofners, and the portrait of Gordon on page three, were taken by Neil Cope. James Cumpsty was responsible for the black and white shots in the section on the Hofner model range at the beginning of the book. James also took the portrait of Neville Marten on page three. Original, early photographs of the Hofner players were generally supplied by the artists themselves. Others were agency or publicity shots.

Dating Hofners
by Paul Day

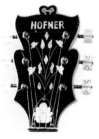

It's nice to know the age of an instrument for two main reasons; firstly to satisfy personal curiosity, and secondly to ascertain value. With many sought-after guitars, the latter aspect is certainly one of the major factors that govern prices. Some Hofners have become collectable in recent years, and so their vintage assumes greater importance. But, as with virtually every guitar mass-manufacturer, it is almost impossible to pinpoint the exact production date of individual examples.

Unlike some brands, Hofner serial number sequences are of little help here, but a number of construction and component changes were made across the range at various times, and these usually provide useful clues as to age. However, please note that all periods shown are approximate, and 'transition' instruments abound, often using various combinations of the features listed.

Adjustable truss-rod in neck: c1960-on

PICKUP TYPE :

1. Fuma-made, six 'star-slot' polepieces.   c1953-59

2. Black, white or brown plastic, plain-top. Oval or square ends.   c1957-60

3. Rectangular metal case, four black slits in top. Hofner 'diamond' logo.   c1960-61

4. Rectangular metal case, six slot-screw OR six rectangular polepieces. Hofner 'diamond' logo on many.   c1961-63

5. Rectangular metal case, six slot-screw PLUS six rectangular polepieces.   c1963-67

6. Rectangular metal case, single central bar-magnet plus six small slot-screw polepieces.   c1967-78

From the late sixties onwards, Hofner introduced various designs based on Fender and Gibson originals, and began using pickups from other manufacturers including Schaller, Shadow and Di Marzio. These have no relevance for dating purposes.

Without Truss Rod Cover - pre 1960

With Truss Rod Cover 1960 on

2. c1957-60

3. c1960-61

4. c1961-63

5. c1963-67

CONTROL LAYOUT

1. Circular panel, body-mounted, with two or four rotary controls. Body-mounted selector toggle-switches where appropriate.   c1957-59

2. Rectangular panel, body or scratchplate-mounted, with one or two rotary controls plus three selector slide-switches. Additional selector switches where appropriate.   c1959-62

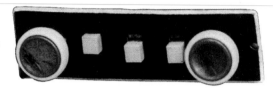

3. Rotary controls, body or scratchplate-mounted. Selector switches as appropriate.   c1962-on

From the late sixties onwards, Hofner introduced various Fender and Gibson based models, with control layouts which closely followed the American originals. In addition there have been numerous new Hofner models, most having specific control layouts. These have no relevance for dating purposes.

The three aspects listed are the only ones common to virtually all Hofner electric guitars produced during the fifties, sixties and seventies. Therefore they are the only ones that can be relied upon to give an accurate indication of production period.

Available Hofner Data

Model	1958	1959	1960	1961	1962	1963	1964	1965	1966	1967	1968	1969	1970	1971
President	3480-5100	–	-7967	7968-	–	8126-8308	8355-	8728-8976	–	–	–	-9002	–	-9027
President Thin	–	–	-681	–	682-	-962	–	1135-	–	–	–	–	–	–
President Flor.	–	–	–	–	–	–	–	–	–	–	-280	–	–	–
Senator	4404-7800	–	-11400	11401-11702	11703-	12080-12680	12726-	13517-13674	-13768	–	–	–	–	–
Senator Thin	–	–	-1088	1089-	1228-	-1404	–	1660-	–	–	–	–	–	–
Senator Bass 1PU	–	-199	200-601	602-	644-	–	–	–	–	–	–	–	–	–
Senator Bass 2PU	–	–	-1020	–	1021-	–	–	–	–	–	–	–	–	–
Congress	5809-7800	–	-9917	9918-10958	10959-12278	12279-13371	13922-	14322-14891	-15141	-15366	-15456	-15471	-15517	-15523
Club 40	255-420	–	-1534	1535-	1675-	–	–	–	–	–	–	–	–	–
Club 50	479-650	–	-1779	1780-	–	–	–	–	–	–	–	–	–	–
Club 60	-180	–	-1296	1297-	1608-	–	–	–	–	–	–	–	–	–
Committee	2564-2950	–	-3677	3721-	3745-	3793-3954	3965-	4109-4177	-4189	-4247	-4258	-4264	–	–
Committee Thin	–	–	-1175	1176-	-1305	1355-1411	1420-	1518-1653	–	–	–	–	–	–
Verithin	–	–	-350	351-	700-1238	1239-2223	2260-	3314	–	–	–	–	–	–
Golden Hofner	–	–	-47	–	–	–	–	–	–	–	–	–	–	–
Golden Thin	–	–	-16	–	–	–	–	–	–	–	–	–	–	–
Vienna	468-700	–	-849	850-	981-	1189-1556	–	1763-2014	-2289	-2414	–	–	-2424	–
Flamenco	4527-5100	–	-5433	5434-5688	5689-6270	6271-7074	7111-	7567-7888	-8338	-8463	-8511	-8556	-8571	-8575

This model and serial number list, whilst obviously incomplete, slightly confusing and almost certainly not 100% accurate, is still a valuable aid to dating Hofners. It looks like records were not kept for 1959, yet numbers had jumped dramatically by 1960.

SOME CONSTRUCTIONAL INFORMATION

Prior to Selmer's distributorship, Hofner did not name their guitars, instead preferring to offer them as model, or order numbers. Serial numbers, too, were non-existent until Selmer's time, although guitars for the European market were numbered later on.

Of Hofner's early guitar range, some models were built from laminated wood – the tops and backs compressed into shape – while others were crafted out of solid timber. By the time Selmer began distribution, all Hofner's semi-acoustics were put together from laminates, for simple reasons of cost. The spruce tops of the expensive archtops were still hand carved from solid planks, and the flamed and birdseye maple veneers used on their backs and rims make them among the most visually stunning guitars ever produced.

Hofner used animal glues to bond tops to rims, rims to backs and necks to bodies. This glue can deteriorate in damp or humid conditions, and a common job for the repairman is to reset necks which have started to come adrift.

One needs only to look at the general detail on Hofner guitars – particularly the inlay work on the more expensive models – to see that it was done by craftsmen, and by hand. One idiosyncrasy of this handwork is that frets are often set inaccurately; either out of parallel to one another or even at slightly incorrect distances. Modern, electronic tuners would probably highlight such discrepancies, but to the human ear they are indiscernible.

The Guitars

Although Selmer's range of Hofners was quite limited, many were offered in both electric and acoustic form, and also in Blonde and Brunette finishes. Hofner's own records show that the 1958 lineup for London consisted of: Committee, President, Senator, Congress, and Clubs 40, 50 and 60. (There were also two nylon-strung acoustics, the Vienna and Flamenco.) '59 saw the introduction of the 500/3 Senator bass, with a Venetian (rounded) cutaway and single pickup. By 1960 the range had been extended to include the Verithin, the President Thin Line, the two-pickup version of the Senator bass (the 500/5, as used by Stu Sutcliffe of The Beatles), the Committee Thin Line, the Golden Hofner (the company's immense and ornate flagship model) and the Golden Thinline. Of this original lineup, only the Congress and Flamenco remained in more or less constant production until the turn of the seventies. According to Hofner's serial number records, the first Congress was numbered 5809, while 1971's final example was stamped 15523.

Committee

Designed by 'a committee of six of Britain's top guitarists', the Committee was big, bold and beautiful. The body measured $20^1/2$" x $17^1/2$" x 3". Beautiful veneers of birdseye maple were used for the back and sides, with black, white and pearloid binding running around all edges, finishing off with

an attractive piped detail on the back. Handsome fingerboard inlays adorned the ebony fingerboard, while a pearl inlaid headstock of magnificent proportions completed the picture. A lyre-style tailpiece and clear, raised finger-rest contributed further to the Committee's air of striking elegance. Early Committee electrics came with black plastic, single coil pickups, while later models conform to the changes detailed in the chapter *Dating Hofners*. Controls comprised: master volume for each pickup, bass and treble boost slide switches and a further slide switch labelled rhythm/solo.

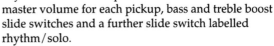

The Committee's most important overall design change came in '63, when the headstock was restyled to bring the guitar more in line with other Hofner models. In the early sixties this fine guitar retailed for around £70!

Golden Hofner

If the Committee was ornate, then the Golden

Hofner, available only in Blonde and produced only during '60 and '61, was nothing short of lush. The Golden's sound box was bigger in all dimensions than that of its close relative, and its edge-binding even more elaborate, with real pearl introduced to add glitz and glitter. Fabulous veneers of quilted maple and contrasting inlay work made the instrument's rear view as interesting, if not more so, than its front. All the Golden

Hofner's hardware was gold plated, with the guitar's *pièce de résistance* its intricately engraved tailpiece. As with the Committee, the Golden's neck was laminated, figured maple. The gold plated machineheads were carved and engraved – miniature works of art in themselves. All this could be bought for a princely 95 gns, complete with fitted case.

President

One of the original Selmer lineup, the President was top of the standard range and based on the same $25^1/2$" scale length as the Golden, Committee, Senator and Congress. According to brochures of the day, the soundboard of the acoustic version was 'hand carved from a block of Bohemian pine'. The rosewood fingerboard was set with Hofner's distinctive 'three dot' arrangement and the headstock inlaid with hand

cut pearl and gold, beneath a Perspex facing. The f-holes were bound with white celluloid and the bridge was the standard archtop variety, adjustable for height via two thumbwheels. The Compensator tailpiece was designed to even out string tension across all six strings. Also available as a Thin Line model, the President Electric was fitted with two pickups and a similar control arrangement to the Committee.

With all Hofner archtops, the Blonde finish was slightly more expensive than the Brunette (or sunburst), since better tops were selected and greater care needed in their lacquering. The acoustic President cost around £30, while the electric version

could be bought for under £50. Many Hofner archtops – the President, Verithin and one or two others – changed to a Florentine (sharp) cutaway later in the sixties, probably due to its more modern appearance. A double Florentine model, the Ambassador, also came out around this time.

Senator

The Senator was the only non-cutaway model in Selmer's regular Hofner range to come in both acoustic and electric form. It was also available as a Thin Line model but, according to Hofner's records, very few of these were shipped. At $20^1/4$" x $16^1/2$" the Senator was slightly smaller than the President and a touch larger than the Congress, the model below it. Looking more like the Gibson company's between-the-wars, economy cello guitars, the Senator was a popular model, with a total 3,300 units (Blonde, Brunette and Electric) being shipped in 1958 alone.

As was the policy with all the better guitar builders, Hofner's middle and lower models lacked mainly ornamentation, rather than basic quality of construction. So the Senator was a fairly plain guitar, using the same bridge and tailpiece as the President, but without that instrument's bound f-holes and 'Hofner' transfer on the body's upper bout. The Senator Electric featured a single pickup (mounted up against the fingerboard) and a slightly simpler control layout (no second volume control).

Congress

This was Selmer's big seller, from '58 all the way through to the early seventies. Even plainer than the Senator, the Congress was nonetheless a serviceable instrument. It was also the guitar on which Hank Marvin founded his career! Available in Brunette only, the Congress featured a 'double dot' rose-wood fingerboard inlaid with brass frets. The bridge and tailpiece were Hofner's standard units. The raised mock-tortoiseshell finger-rest extended from the 16th fret right up to the bridge. Like all Hofner's archtops, the neck of the Congress joined its body at the 14th fret.

In 1960, Hofner introduced truss rods on their guitars, the three-screw cover on the headstock allowing easy access, should adjustment be necessary. As the inclusion of truss rods allowed the necks to be made thinner and more playable, Hofner invented the term 'Slendanek', which it applied with great gusto to all its instruments from that point onwards.

In 1960 the Congress cost around £15, which was probably the average man's weekly wage.

Club 50 and Club 40

For many players the most enduring and loved of all Hofner's original model lineup, these little guitars were light and immensely friendly to play – notwithstanding the thick necks of the early models. When amplified, the Club exhibited a strong, warm tone which made it the perfect rhythm guitar.

Differing only by the 50's extra pickup at the bridge, these two Club models were of laminated construction throughout, with spruce veneered tops and plain maple backs and rims. The necks were also maple but with a central reinforcement strip of beech. Early Club 40s and 50s came with a vertical Hofner headstock logo, but this was soon changed to the 'stave and treble clef' motif found on various other models at around the same time. The scratchplate of the 40 and 50 was a simple, mock tortoiseshell affair, raised from the body by a bracket on the rim, but also attached to the bridge and neck by a simple pin arrangement. The fingerboards of these models were unbound rosewood, and the dot position markers completed a plain but workmanlike impression. As with other Hofner models, the pickups and various items of hardware were subject to change over the years, but the classic Clubs are the black pickup models pictured here.

All Clubs were based on a scale length of $25^3/8"$ and prices began at under £30 for the Club 40.

Club 60

The Club 60 arrived in late 1958, hot on the heels of the 40 and 50. But the 60 was a very different animal, certainly in appearance. Laden with pearl inlays along the ebony fingerboard and on the bound headstock, featuring highly figured maple for the back and rims and boasting pearloid scratchplate and control panel, the Club 60 was a stunner. Available in Blonde or a fetching Cherry Sunburst the 60 was the model you wanted, but probably couldn't afford, at over £40! A Club 70 made a brief appearance in 1968,

as an improved version of the 60.

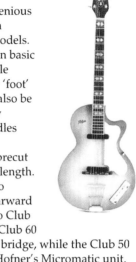

The Clubs featured an ingenious bridge arrangement which Hofner used on various models. Although fairly standard in basic design – a height-adjustable bridge sitting on an ebony 'foot' – the Clubs' bridge could also be adjusted for intonation, by setting the individual saddles (actually short lengths of fretwire) into one of four precut slots running the bridge's length. A forward slot was used to sharpen the note and a rearward slot to flatten it. Of the two Club guitars pictured here, the Club 60 is fitted with the standard bridge, while the Club 50 has been modified using Hofner's Micromatic unit.

Some years later, stockpiled Club bodies were fitted with Beatle bass necks in an attempt to keep up with demand for that model. The truth was that people wanted the violin body, a fact underlined by poor sales of the hybrid.

Verithin

Measuring a mere 3mm ($1^1/4"$) at the rim, the Verithin was the slimmest semi-acoustic guitar around. Featuring a braced spruce top and a fine maple veneered back the Verithin was a wholly hollow guitar, unlike Gibson's ES335 on which it was probably modelled. It was also surprisingly loud when played acoustically.

First arriving on the scene in 1960, the early Verithins came with the elegant pickups seen on this example and the same control panel and layout as found on most archtop and semi-acoustic Hofners. The headstock was that of the Club 60, but the fingerboard, with its lateral pearloid and tortoiseshell-striped markers, was entirely new. The standard Verithin featured a handsome trapeze tailpiece, but was also available with a Bigsby vibrato unit as an extra cost option. The Verithin boasted 22 frets, but playing above the 15th was tricky, due to the guitar's intrusive heel. The Verithin stayed in production throughout the sixties, after which time it was replaced with various models which sought to copy Gibson's successful semi-acoustic range, but which never possessed the personality of this very fine, very thin guitar.

500/1 Beatle Bass

The Beatle Bass was only so dubbed after the group's massive impact and the fact that Paul McCartney chose to play one. The famous 'thumbs up' tag featuring a smiling Beatle Paul greeted the thousands who flocked to buy this interesting instrument. Various changes occurred over the years, mostly in line with those which were taking place on other Hofner instruments – truss rods, pickup modifications, etc. The Beatle bass highlighted the separation of identities between German and British Hofners. Initially not available here as a Selmer model, Paul bought his violin basses while the band were in Germany, and it was only added to the UK model range after the band's fame had erupted in 1963.

More detailed information on Beatle basses is contained in the Paul McCartney interview in the *Hofner Players* section. Note the two different model basses being played by Paul.

Semi-acoustic Basses

At one time or another Hofner produced bass versions of most of their semi-acoustic and archtop guitars. These used the same bodies, pickups and controls as the guitars, and Hofner simply added bass necks and repositioned the bridges accordingly. Included among these instruments were the Committee Bass, the President Bass, the Senator Bass (originally called simply the 'Hofner Bass Guitar' by Selmer) and the Verithin Bass. The Senator Bass is the instrument which Stu Sutcliffe, the original bass player in The Beatles, played. The story goes that Sutcliffe, a brilliant artist, sold a painting for £65 and, in order to join the band, blew the lot on the bass in Hessy's music shop in Liverpool.

HOFNER SOLID GUITARS

The Colorama

Although this book is more concerned with Hofner's archtops and semi-acoustics, a number of solid models came out of the Bubenreuth factory. The early solids included the Coloramas. These came in many different forms; with both single and double cutaway bodies;

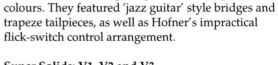

with both one or two pickups; and in many solid colours. They featured 'jazz guitar' style bridges and trapeze tailpieces, as well as Hofner's impractical flick-switch control arrangement.

Super Solids: V1, V2 and V3

The Super Solids of the early sixties were the vaguely Stratocasterish V1, V2 and V3, with either one, two or three humbucking pickups. The Supers were fitted with bolt-on maple necks. The rosewood fingerboard of the V-range was inlaid with double dot markers, as opposed to the Colorama's single dot arrangement. Pickup selection was via a switch on the lower horn and the controls were still Hofner's archaic flick-switches. The tremolo system, too, fell a long way short of what Fender had achieved and so the guitars lacked the stage usability of 'equivalent' American instruments. The V-models were later improved and became the Super 2 and Super 3, with more sensible control layout and also featuring the Verithin's (and the Galaxie's) striped fingerboard inlays. A two pickup bass version of the Super was called the Artist.

At around £50 the Supers were still inexpensive compared to the American guitars of the time, so many British players bought Super Solids and Coloramas out of necessity, at which time the desire was born to upgrade to a Fender or Gibson as soon as possible.

Like their archtops and semi-acoustics, Hofner's solid guitars spawned bass versions. Again, they paled by comparison to their American counterparts and so, other than stepping stones towards Fender Precisions and Jazz Basses, their position in guitar development is relatively unimportant.

Galaxie

"Made to give all the effects and variety of tone colour that today's music demands" read the blurb for Hofner's top of the range solid, the Galaxie. Arriving later on in the sixties the Galaxie boasted three Nova Sonic humbucking pickups, each with adjacent on/off switch and tone control wheel. A master volume wheel was sited by the neck. Hofner's new tremolo bridge with flick-down damper was fitted, obviously in mind of Fender's Jaguar and Jazzmaster models. The Galaxie was a very flashy guitar, finished in bright red, with striped inlays and black-faced, six-a-side headstock. However, it was complex to operate and, again, could not compete with the simplicity of its American rivals. The Galaxie retailed at 55gns – just over £60.

Hofner Electric Guitars And Basses 1965-2009
By Paul Day

The previous section concentrates on those Hofner models that appeared during the 1950s and early-1960s. The following provides information on some of the many other electric guitars and basses subsequently produced by the company, up to and including the present day.

1960s

Called the Club series in the UK, Hofner's small-bodied semi-acoustics had been very successful since their introduction in the mid-1950s. In 1965, Hofner finally decided to add a bass version, the 500/2, which was never officially imported here, but proved popular in America. Apart from the single-cutaway shape, it was identical to the equivalent-period 500/1 model, including scale length and control configuration.

Also debuting that year was the 4575: the most comprehensively equipped version of Hofner's super-slim, semi-acoustic design known as the Verithin in Britain. The new addition featured the same shallow, Gretsch-influenced twin cutaways, but three pickups partnered a trio of slide-switch selectors located on the left horn, while a row of controls was accommodated on a long curving panel down below.

During this decade many Hofner six-string solids echoed the styling of Fender's Stratocaster or Jazz Bass, but more upmarket models introduced during the latter half of the 1960s tended to favour this US maker's Jazzmaster in terms of body shape, as it was very popular in Europe at the time. The 177 Exquisite (pictured) and 178 Grande Surprise were just two such examples, each offering something special in the way of circuitry, such as multi switch

selectors, sliders and Hofner's 'Organ Effect' sprung-return roller swell control.

Hofner eventually cashed in on the success of their 500/1 violin bass by issuing a guitar version in 1966. Construction and components of the 459 were suitably similar, while options included a vibrato tailpiece and active electronics offering built-in tone boosts and fuzz. The 459 Super was a deluxe alternative featuring gold-plated metalwork.

Slimline semi-acoustics such as Gibson's ES-330 were favoured by many 1960s guitarists and the 4572 from 1969 was unsurprisingly similar in construction with its twin-cutaway body styling. The pickup configuration and circuitry were equally alike, although Hofner chose not to copy the actual Gibson control layout.

1970s

This was the decade when copying well-known US original instruments was considered the most commercial method of manufacture. Hofner agreed that imitation was the sincerest form of flattery and during the first half of the 1970s they accordingly produced a succession of surrogate Fenders and Gibsons. The former was represented by six-string solids such as the 170, 175 and 179, which were respective reproductions of the Stratocaster, Telecaster and Jazzmaster. The 174 (pictured) simulated Gibson's familiar SG, while the 4579 (pictured) was a Les Paul look-alike, also available in HiFi form, featuring upgraded pickups that employed unusual wooden covers. Less obvious impersonations were the 166 and 171 models, which mimicked the Gibson L-6S and Fender's Telecaster Thinline respectively. Popular basses also provided easy targets, including the Gibson EB-styled 187 and the Fender Jazz-inspired 189.

Hofner's return to original thinking in the latter 1970s was ably represented by the Razorwood series of solids. Launched in 1978, this line comprised 6- and 12-string examples, plus a matching bass, each sharing the same unusual styling, natural finish, and all-mahogany construction. Humbucking pickups were standard throughout, governed by control circuitry that came in a variety of passive or active configurations.

In marked contrast, the S5PA was a straightforward looking, single-cutaway solid, with a somewhat stolid-looking, broad body that, like the glued-in neck, was natural-finished mahogany. Described by Hofner in 1978 as "the ultimate rock guitar", it paired twin humbuckers with an on-board active preamp intended to overdrive any amp input.

The S5E employed the same silhouette, although this conventional outline contradicted comprehensive and complex circuitry. Also introduced in 1978, this six-string's appearance may have seemed Gibsonesque, but a trio of single-coils supplied distinctly Fender-flavoured sounds, enhanced by active electronics that incorporated a 5-brand graphic equaliser, plus a sensitivity switch and multi-position preset selection system.

Hofner's archtop heritage hadn't been forgotten, thanks to new models such as the A2L (pictured), which appeared in 1978. This big-bodied, single-cutaway jazzer featured flamed maple sides and back partnering a spruce front. Simple volume and tone controls governed a fingerboard-mounted humbucker, but a piezo pickup-equipped bridge and stereo output were optional extras.

Debuting in 1979, the T4S semi-acoustic maintained the combination of the company's classic twin-shallow cutaway styling and deeper body of the T2S, first seen the previous year. The latter came with optional active circuitry, but this was standard on its newer stablemate, including 3-band EQ that partnered two humbuckers and coil-switching facilities.

1980s

First seen in 1980, the T6S (pictured) was another six-string that employed Hofner's popular super-slim depth body format and long-established shallow twin-cutaway shape. Construction was actually semi-solid, featuring a central sustain block and no f-holes. Pickup configuration varied, as did control layout and circuitry, the latter being passive or active, including an optional piezo-equipped bridge/tailpiece.

By this time, the through-neck, multi-laminate wood construction pioneered by Alembic in the US was influencing makers elsewhere and Hofner was no exception. The S9C appeared in 1980, sporting twin-horned styling on a suitably stripy, maple and bubinga body. Humbuckers were the norm by this time, with a pair partnering circuitry that included coil-switching, active 3-band EQ and an on-board compressor.

The S11 Heavy Duty (pictured) debuted the next year, boasting an original angular body shape that, like this model's name, suggested a heavy metal image. However, Hofner described it as 'an exquisite country rock guitar', partnering two Super Distortion humbuckers with a piezo-loaded bridge/tailpiece that supplied pseudo-acoustic sounds.

Added in 1982, the three-strong Venture series maintained the multi-wood, through-necked formula of the S9C and Heavy Duty. However, the various Ventures featured more familiar styling, with the E and V (pictured) versions respectively echoing Gibson's Explorer and Flying V designs, while the Venture S took its cue straight from the Fender Stratocaster. Pickups and control layouts stayed equally true to their inspirations and all three combined brass hardware with a natural wood finish.

Travel-type instruments were quite trendy around this time and starting in 1982, the Shorty series represented Hofner's attempt to grab a share of the market for 'go anywhere' electrics. The guitar combined a full-size neck with a minimalist body and the bass was suitably short-scale. Like the latter, the Shorty Standard six-string featured a single humbucker and simple circuitry, while its Super equivalent added a built-in amplifier and speaker for optional self-contained operation. These little cuties came in a variety of colours and were re-named Hofner Choppers for the UK market.

The S2 solid series comprised two guitars and a bass, all adopting a no-nonsense attitude via offset-cutaway, chunky mahogany bodies in natural finish, bolt-on maple necks, predictable pickups, straightforward circuitry and panel-mounted controls. However, the S2A broke this basic mould by incorporating a built-in 2W amplifier and twin speakers.

One of Hofner's more eye-catching six-string solids was introduced in 1985. The inventive body shape of the Alpha (pictured) promoted a rock-conscious image, as did the reversed headstock and locking vibrato system. A single-coil and humbucker pickup combination was governed by clever circuitry that included individual outputs. A Custom version offered various options, such as differing hardware.

Debuting in 1987, the Reference range of six-string solidbodies was equally rock-oriented and represented a concerted attempt by the company to keep pace with changing market trends. The first Reference models combined Telecaster-type styling with various, more original ideas on pickups, circuitry and hardware, the latter including a choice of locking vibrato systems. The line was augmented four years later by the addition of a similarly varying selection of suitably equipped, Stratocaster-styled alternatives (pictured).

Alongside all this solidbody innovation, the company also continued to cater to far more conventional tastes. Named after noted German guitarist Attila Zoller, the AZ (pictured) appeared in 1982. This archtop acoustic-electric combined flamed maple construction with a solid spruce top, while a bound rosewood fingerboard boasted split-block position markers. A floating Attila Zoller pickup accompanied

body-mounted controls and a carved wooden pickguard. The alternative AZ Award added an ebony fingerboard and gold-plated metalwork.

The Attila Zoller Fusion model (pictured) added in 1989 matched its title by adopting a more modern approach. Construction still combined spruce with flamed maple, but incorporated a centre sustain block. The body carried two AZ humbuckers plus a control quartet and selector switch, while a six-saddle bridge partnered a fine tuner tailpiece.

The aptly named Jazzica single-cutaway archtop-acoustic was launched in 1989 and incorporated some novel features. The body was tapered, doubling in depth from neck end to base, while the bound rosewood fingerboard featured 24 frets and pearl block position markers. Twin streamlined soundholes partnered a floating AZ pickup, body-mounted controls and gold-plated metalwork.

In 1986 the Nightingale revived the copycat theme, being very obviously based on Gibson's ES-335 slimline semi in terms of styling and construction. The bridge and tailpiece were similarly derivative; likewise the twin humbuckers and attendant control layout, although the circuitry included stereo outputs. The Nightingale Custom offered various hardware choices and added a master volume, the latter also being employed on the Special version added four years later.

1990s

Commissioned by a leading UK retailer in 1994, the limited edition 500/1 Cavern Bass re-created the original 1961 version of Hofner's venerable violin-shaped four-string, as played by Beatle Paul McCartney in the band's formative years. Specifications were as accurate as possible, including appropriately correct construction, pickup type and positioning, headstock logo and hardware.

That same year saw Hofner bring out an upmarket Sixties reissue under their own steam, in the form of the Vintage '63 model (pictured). This employed period-correct construction and components, including wide-spaced pickups and old-style control panel. A Vintage '62 version was added in 1995, while the following year brought an appropriate 40th Anniversary edition, although somewhat surprisingly, this didn't re-create the original 1956 design.

2000s

By the start of the New Millennium, Hofner had been under the aegis of Boosey & Hawkes for six years. Since being acquired by this company Hofner had moved to a new factory and production policy had also changed. This was reflected by the 2000 catalogue, which concentrated solely on more traditional designs.

As indicated by its title, the Verythin Classic harked back to the 1960s Verithin, but with updated construction and improved components. The Vice President came equally close to the original but while the New President (pictured) also hinted at the past, this archtop-electric was very different from its predecessor, featuring a floating humbucker and pickguard-mounted controls.

The latest Hofner line still concentrates on looking to the past for inspiration and, although the Chancellor (pictured) is a new archtop-electric, this flagship model is very much in the traditional mould.

The Thin President succeeds the Vice President, while the three-pickup-equipped Verythin Evolution 3 is an updated derivation of the 4575 six-string from 1965. Reissues now figure more prominently and having re-created the Club 40, as played by embryonic

Beatle John Lennon, Hofner now offer an accurate reincarnation of the Club 50 from the late 1950s. Similarly, the 500/1 50th Anniversary Bass offered in 2006 commemorated five decades of Hofner's most famous four-string, but like the 40th Anniversary edition this didn't attempt to re-create the original design. Instead, that honour has been reserved for the 2009 limited edition Vintage '58 version. Another recent addition on the four-string front is the 500/2 Club Bass, which authentically revives the 1965 model.

The Chinese-sourced CT line offers more-affordable alternatives to Hofner's German-made models, some being closer imitations than others. The Club emulates the original, but employs semi-solid construction, while the gold-fronted Club GT (pictured) adds revised hardware, pickups and circuitry. The similarly styled Club Bass is a semi-solid equivalent of the recent reissue in the German range, while the equally cost-conscious Violin Bass also uses a solid centre section.

The Verythin combines the shape of the original with Gibson-influenced electrics, while the new Verythin 60's style version appropriately offers more period-related features plus a Bigsby vibrato tailpiece. The equally recent Verythin 3 (pictured) is a variation sporting triple pickups and a suitable switch panel.

The diminutive Shorty six-string (pictured) is re-created quite accurately, but in contrast, the Colorama Custom and Special don't directly resemble anything from Hofner's past, being more Gibsonish twin-cutaway solids, respectively equipped with twin humbuckers and a pair of P90-type single-coils.

The Hofner Guitar Company History

The influences of American rock 'n' roll music began to spread to other countries during the 1950s. West Germany felt the effects before many parts of Europe, thanks to the large contingent of US armed forces still stationed there after the end of World War II. As the popularity of this new music style grew, so did the numbers of German guitarists keen to imitate and emulate the American originators. The guitars played by the stars were hard to find outside the US, and were very expensive, so German makers needed to come up with their own equivalents.

Hofner realised the commercial potential of the fast-growing electric guitar market before many of their competitors. The company had been founded during the late 1880s in Schoenbach by German violin maker Karl Hofner (pictured) and initially produced violins, cellos, and double basses, Acoustic guitars weren't added until 1925. By this time, sons Josef and Walter had joined their father's business, which had become one of the largest in the area.

After the Second World War the Hofner family moved to Moehrendorf, near Erlangen. Manufacture re-commenced in 1949, but two years later the company re-located to a new factory in Bubenreuth, which became home to Hofner for more than four decades.

Archtop acoustic guitars were introduced during the early 1950s, soon being partnered by electrified equivalents. Purpose-built electric six-strings, with built-in pickups and controls, were being produced by 1954, their integral type construction pre-dating much of Hofner's homegrown competition. These models varied from big-bodied jazzers to scaled-down instruments that represented this maker's answer to the Gibson Les Paul, albeit hollow and

therefore much lighter. Actual solids arrived in 1956, although these also had air inside, as did the first Hofner bass, which boasted a violin-shaped body.

The early electrics soon found their way to the UK and it wasn't long before the brand was featuring prominently on the music scene in Britain, providing hundreds of hopeful guitar heroes with their first stepping-stone six-strings.

In addition to the mushrooming beginner market, many British pro players also relied on the guitars from this major German manufacturer, as it was a time when choice was severely limited on the home front, thanks to an embargo on American imports, still in force after World War II. The ban was lifted at the start of the 1960s, but Hofner continued to enjoy great success in the face of greater competition, faring appreciably better than German rivals such as Framus, Hopf and Hoyer. This level of popularity was due in no small part to the efforts of the company's UK importers, Selmer.

all makers elsewhere in the world felt the adverse effects of this quite sudden cold wind of commercial change. The transition towards 'rock' music also contributed to Hofner's unexpected international decline, not helped by a seeming reluctance to move with the musical times in terms of instrument design.

The company fared no better than most contemporary competitors and struggled to retain a fair share of an ever more-competitive and increasingly American-minded market. Sales were further hit when the Japanese copy invasion hit the electric guitar industry hard during the 1970s.

This London-based distributor had been doing well with the brand since 1953, offering from Hofner's sizeable range a small selection that later included variations specifically made or modified for export to the UK. Selmer's marketing efforts helped to build a strong brand identity, with all models available here being allocated image-inducing actual names, rather than the usual number designations favoured by Hofner, which tended to be less interesting and more confusing.

In the early 1960s, Hofner accordingly maintained a healthy share of the burgeoning beat-group market thank to an expanded catalogue. Many models now targeted both first- and second-time buyers, offering affordable alternatives for those aspiring to own big name American instruments but lacking the necessary and appreciable extra funds. Although not up to Fender or Gibson levels in terms of quality, Hofner electrics embodied character, often-impressive appearance and performance abilities that met the needs of their intended audience.

In the boom times of the early 1960s, Hofner electrics owed some obvious design debts to the best-selling American originals, but the company never felt the need to resort to blatant copycatting, preferring instead to absorb and adapt the influences exerted on the market by Fender and Gibson.

This policy was forcibly altered dramatically during the next decade, when the Japanese guitar industry realised the money that could be made by providing more-affordable and apparently close approximations of the most popular US electrics. Almost overnight, guitar markets around the world became saturated with a flood of facsimiles, all intended to catch the eyes, if not the ears, of the playing public, and offered at temptingly low prices. This combination was hard to ignore and virtually every maker in the West soon felt the financial pinch, as increasing numbers of potential customers were captivated by this invasion of imitations.

Popularity peaked later in the decade, helped in no small way by Beatle Paul McCartney's high profile use of his Hofner 'violin' bass. At this time, the company enjoyed appropriately healthy export sales throughout Europe and in the UK, while America proved to be another lucrative market.

In marked contrast to this highly encouraging growth, Hofner's share of the market diminished significantly during the latter half of the decade, a period when the majority of players switched their attention and allegiances to electrics made in the USA. Virtually

Hofner certainly didn't escape this dramatic downturn, as sales at home and abroad shrank with startling rapidity. It seemed everyone wanted copies and, like other German makers, Hofner had to respond to this demand to stand some chance of survival. It was very much a case of "if you can't beat 'em, join 'em", and in 1970 the company's existing catalogue of originals was accordingly augmented by a selection of six- and four-string models that made no secret of their Fender or Gibson inspirations and aspirations.

While Selmer may have long since realised the commercial benefits of bestowing names to models, Hofner had yet to cotton on and still preferred to play the numbers game. This meant that, with very few exceptions, the instruments continued to employ a confusing and boring digits-only system, although of course it could've proved difficult to come up with suitable new original titles for such obvious copycats.

However, while Japanese makers went to great lengths to make their mimics at least look pretty much like the real thing, for whatever reason, Hofner and other German manufacturers opted to offer more approximate interpretations, rather than straight fakes. This allowed them to incorporate some of their

Hofner tradition or revived earlier designs, although in reality only the continually produced 'Beatle' basses attracted the most consistent and greatest interest.

In 1994, Hofner was bought by British company Boosey & Hawkes, and three years later the factory moved from Bubenreuth to a new facility near neighbouring Hagenau. Since then the range has been rationalised and revitalised, augmented by a Chinese-made line that comprises more-affordable equivalents of old favourites along with some all-new ideas. The current German catalogue offers both flattop and archtop acoustics, while electrics include high-end authentic vintage reissues plus updated interpretations of earlier Hofner classics. Basses naturally still feature strongly via various versions of the ever-popular violin model and other four-strings.

own ideas on design, which in turn usually restricted their attempts to accurately ape the originals. It should also be said that these departures often tended to impair rather than improve the end results in both looks and performance.

This somewhat stubborn policy must have similarly hindered sales, especially in the face of the far more familiar-looking Far Eastern fakes, but this didn't seem to deter Hofner. Not surprisingly, their attempts at imitation fared badly compared to the success enjoyed by the Japanese-origin opposition and did little to stem the swing towards the latter.

Despite doubts previously expressed to the contrary, Hofner are still very much in business. These days, the wheel has turned almost full circle, as the product line primarily concerns traditional stringed instruments. On the guitar side, the company still tends to concentrate on creating electrics that echo the better times in Hofner history. These are undeniably superior to the oldie originals in terms of construction, performance and playability, which certainly bodes well for the future of this, the most famous of all German guitar brands.

Even so, unlike many rivals, Hofner managed to survive what were lean times, subsequently soldiering on at a much lower market level. The brand's profile outside Germany diminished accordingly, to the point where many players thought the company had long since ceased production!

The line of look-alikes had failed to reverse the downward sales trend, so by the late 1970s the company reverted to more original thinking, while build quality actually improved, becoming significantly better than that of earlier eras.

Numerous new models were introduced during the 1980s and into the next decade. Some reflected changing trends in terms of construction and components, while others stuck strictly with

The Hofner Players

Thoughts and memories from some of the many guitar greats who were influenced or inspired by Hofner guitars.

Hank B. Marvin

Hilary Giltrap

In 1958 a father from the North of England made a purchase that was to revolutionise British pop music: Mr.Marvin bought his son Hank a Hofner Congress guitar...

"That was 1958, and I had the guitar when I joined a band called The Railroaders. I think it cost sixteen guineas at the time and it was a simple acoustic. I then bought a pickup which fastened to the end of the fingerboard - one of those dreadful, metal, square ones with strange little pole pieces on, and a wire coming away from it, straight into the amp."

History reminds us that Hank teamed up with his Newcastle buddy, guitarist Bruce Welch and two other friends to form The Drifters. This band was soon to become The Shadows, the inventive bass of Jet Harris and the exceptional drumming of Tony Meehan having replaced original members, Terry Smart and Ian Samwell. The group was Cliff Richard's backing band until 1968, but also had a string of hits under its own name, including Number Ones 'Apache', 'Kon-Tiki', 'Wonderful Land', 'Dance On' and 'Foot Tapper'. But back in his

Hofner Congress days Hank didn't even own an amplifier...

"Someone either gave or lent me an amp. It was about as big as a large cornflake packet; it was a funny little thing, looked like an old radio. It was only a little amplifier and it wasn't very loud, and if you turned it up to any level it just distorted like mad. But nevertheless I can still recall that first thrill of hearing my own amplified guitar."

History was very nearly rewritten when Marvin almost electrocuted himself with his 'dreadful little pickup' and 'cornflake packet' amp.

"I hadn't had the pickup on very long when we did a week at the Palace in Newcastle. It was strange, not having any understanding or knowledge of electric guitars, amplifiers, or even electricity, to touch the microphone and not realise quite what I'd done. There was a bang and a flash and the strings were actually all burned on the edges, and I really did think, 'Crumbs, is that what happens every time you break a string on an electric guitar?' Then the electrician came running over, white-faced, and told me what had happened. Fortunately I wasn't touching the guitar; I just had it hanging in front of me, turned round to say something and it swung round and the strings hit the mic."

Although more than pleased with his Congress, Hank felt the Committee, as played by Skiffle star Tommy Steele, was really the last word in guitars in 1958. It's rumoured that Steele's guitar was specially made, with golden frets, such was Tommy's influence and status... "Yes... Tommy Steele's guitar... with all the purfling and inlays on it. But back then you just wanted to look at guitars and imagine owning one and being a good player. I thought the Committee just looked wonderful, whereas the Congress was a very simple, plain instrument. Even so, I was still knocked out to have it because it was my own guitar. I was in a skiffle group before we joined The Railroaders, and the piano player in the band had an old guitar that he let me borrow. I learned a few chords on it and used to double on banjo and guitar - very impressive in those days! So when I joined the Railroaders I already had the Congress."

Hank, left, with his Hofner Congress.

"I've been trying to think what happened to that guitar. I think I eventually gave it to someone. The singer in The Railroaders lent me a black Vega and said, 'You use this, it's a proper electric guitar with a good sound'. So I used the Vega all the time and when we came to London I was using it down at the 'Two Is' club. I still had the Congress, but it was lying around and I wasn't using it, because it wasn't really good enough by then. So I probably gave it to someone. It would be worth more than a couple of quid now, though, but you don't think of that; no-one anticipates a thing like that

ever being of any value."

The playability of guitars in those formative years of British pop music was a fairly hit and miss affair. Guitarists often had little understanding of their instrument's workings and Hank was no exception...

"I used Cathedral strings and they would stay on until they broke or rusted away. I knew nothing about the practical side of guitars, apart from lowering and raising the action: the Congress had two adjustment wheels on either side of the bridge, so I used those to get the strings as low as I could without buzzing. No-one seemed to know anything about that sort of thing then, whereas today there's a guitar maintenance man on every street corner. Back then, we were stuck with what we got." (On the album sleeve of the LP 'The Shadows' a piece of rolled up paper is clearly visible in the fifth string nut slot of Marvin's Fender Stratocaster, where the string's height had been adjusted too low, probably by Hank himself).

"But there was plenty of mystery in those days. We didn't know anything about adjusting the truss rod or generally setting up - you lowered the action until it felt good, and if there was a buzz you raised it again. Pretty primitive stuff."

The Congress was the only Hofner owned by Marvin. Of course Hank eventually became synonymous with the Fender Stratocaster, apart from a period in the sixties when The Shadows switched allegiance to the guitars of the 'British Leo Fender'Jim Burns.

"But that Hofner Congress has fond memories, because my Dad bought it for me and because it was actually mine, and I could take it home after a gig and listen to something on the radio and try to work out the chords, or the sax solo, or try to play the tunes that the singer was singing."

In order to jog a few memories, a 1958 Congress, exactly like the one purchased by Marvin's father, is produced. Hank smiles and examines the guitar closely and with care...

"You know I'd forgotten they had a zero fret. And look, there are the little wheels for adjusting the bridge. But look at the height of that action - you could shoot arrows with that.. !"

Jim Sullivan

Probably the most famous session guitarist of the sixties 'Big Jim' Sullivan's first serious gig was with Marty Wilde's Wildcats. Jim remained in demand as a studio musician and was later to tour the world and record with Tom Jones in the seventies and the incredibly successful German orchestra leader James Last in the eighties.

One of his first inspirations, though, was Denny Wright, the influential jazz guitarist who added flair and spice to the recordings of Skiffle stars Lonny Donegan and Johnny Duncan.

"Denny had a Hofner Committee," recalls Jim, "and that's what I wanted." Of course, money was tight during the fifties; rationing was still in force in Britain and the price of a Committee was a King's ransom for a lad from Hounslow. So Sullivan's first guitar was a Framus Black Rose, after which he acquired a Hofner Senator.

"I got the Senator from a music shop in Hounslow, but never got round to having a Committee," he muses, "even though it has always been one of my favourite guitars. After the Senator I got a Maton, an Australian guitar, which was beautiful. It had a carved top, and when I say carved, it was really carved. Absolutely beautifully made."

"But I did actually use a Committee on a session in the early 60s, with Johnny Duncan. It was just after Denny Wright had left the band when I did a couple of the tracks with Johnny; I also played with him on the road for a while; we did the American camps and things like that. I was using a Gibson Les Paul by then, but that wasn't the required sound and so the old Hofner Committee came out. It was Johnny's Committee, though, not mine."

"And Tony Belcher with the Wildcats had a Hofner Club, with the little black pickups. They were beautiful guitars, very neat, and Tony got a great sound out of it. But the Committee was the inspirational guitar, and the only one that looked like it did, with that big headstock and all the frills and all the inlays."

British rock'n'roller Joe Brown states emphatically that the Hofner guitar shaped the sound of British rock'n'roll. Jim Sullivan agrees, although adds a suggestion of his own...

"I think it's true to a certain extent, because Hofners were the crème de là crème, the best guitars available here before the American instruments started to come over. But actually the first solid guitar that I ever saw was an Antoria, and I had one of those when I was with Marty Wilde; I think it was the same as the one Hank Marvin had, because Hank had an Antoria prior to his Strat. It was a funny-looking shape and the pickups were so microphonic; I mean, you could tap anywhere on the guitar and it would come through. We used that on 'Wilde About Marty'."

"But we were all groping to find something back then. And Tony Sheridan (the singer who later recorded with The Beatles) had a Strat-looking Grazioso guitar. I've no idea where he got it from and I've never seen one since. It was the first solid guitar that I'd seen, other than a Fender Telecaster. And the sound Sheridan got in '56/'57 was, to me, the beginning of rock'n'roll, because all of us kids in those days had our full-bodied guitars. When I joined Marty, he had a Gibson Les Paul that he'd got from Sister Rosetta Tharp, an American blues/gospel singer. Then, when they started importing Gibsons, I got the first Gibson cherry red Stereo guitar (ES345) in the country. That cost me nearly £300 in 1959 or 1960; I walked

into Ivor Mairants' shop, saw it hanging up on the wall, and... Wow!"

"But I felt the guitars Hofner made after the Committee and the Club never really retained their originality. The Committee was entirely its own thing, and Denny Wright got his own sound out of that, whether electrically or acoustically."

"My trouble was that when I joined Marty I went straight on to a solid, either Marty's Gibson or my Antoria - in fact I only had the Antoria for about three weeks and then Marty brought out the Gibson so I had that from then on. So I was playing the Gibson Les Paul, which was heaven. It was like, 'Cor, what is that.?!!"'

"And of course then Hofner themselves groped around to try and cover all these other areas, bringing out the Verithin to copy the Gibson 335 and the Galaxie, which was a sort of Strat copy. So I think they lost a lot of their originality."

"But Hofner was certainly the name on everybody's lips in those days. It was the guitar. It was the guitar my idol was playing at the time; I loved Donegan and Johnny Duncan, and Denny Wright played with both of them and it's a pity that Denny never got the recognition that he deserves in British guitar playing, because he certainly inspired a lot of us kids. He used to stand up there with this big Hofner Committee and blast out these notes; they used to come out like great big pebbles, the notes from that guitar. Denny had a kind of jazz approach; it wasn't rock'n'roll, it was jazz, Latin-jazz."

Along with most Hofner players of the period, Big Jim is vague about the fate of his Senator...

"I more than likely gave it away. I ended up at one time with nearly 40 guitars that I hung on to over a period of years and they were all in the cupboard gathering dust, so I gave them away. I sold a few, gave a few away and lent a few to people, never got them back and can't remember who I even lent them to."

Hilary Giltrap

Paul McCartney

Of all the Hofner players of the sixties one stands out. Not just because his Hofner was a bass; not just because his playing was left handed; but because he was Paul McCartney, founder member of the band that changed the world, The Beatles. The bass was Hofner's 500/1 Violin bass.

Walter Hofner, son of the original founder and an accomplished violin maker himself, had conceived the idea of producing a bass guitar in the shape of a bass viol. So, reducing the bass viol's shape, fitting it with a guitar style neck and specially designed strings, the Violin bass was unveiled at the German Music Fair of 1956.

"I got my Violin bass in Hamburg, at the shop in the town centre," recalls Paul; "I seem to remember it cost the German Mark equivalent of thirty quid or so, which was about two weeks' wages in those days! I've got a feeling it came with a sort of semi-hard case, but it couldn't have been anything very effective because it didn't last long. I think I had the first one nicked, so I don't really know what happened to that - we'll keep an eye out for it, in case it shows up somewhere."

The 'Beatle Bass', as it was soon dubbed by

fans, originally had pickups designed as oval shaped pendants of ebony, into which the coils and magnets were sunk. These were initially both sited by the end of the fingerboard, although the second pickup was soon moved nearer the bridge for greater tonal variation.

The oval control plate of early models was also changed to the better-known rectangular version, and the tailpiece shortened to that seen on later basses. In 1961 Hofner developed more efficient, metal-cased pickups and added the company name to the headstock. This is the instrument most associated with Paul McCartney. By 1966 the pickups had evolved into the version featuring four adjustable screws and four magnetic blocks. The pickups were redesigned yet again in 1968 and known as style 513B.

The Beatles purchased their Hofners at Steinway's shop in Hamburg...

"On the second floor of the Steinway shop they had guitars rather than pianos," recalls Paul, "and John bought a Club 40 there when I got my bass. That was before he got his Rickenbacker. And I've got an idea maybe George got one as well. But certainly John did."

During the 'Beatlemania' years demand for the 500/1 grew to the stage where the factory was unable to keep up with the demand. However they refused to change either the design or the production methods just to achieve increased sales, instead continuing to craft each instrument by hand.

McCartney still owns and uses the replacement for his stolen original. He also has one backup 500/1.

"The main one I use is one of the originals. I still use it a lot, actually; it was Elvis Costello who got me to get it out of mothballs. It was a little inaccurate in the tuning, particularly up at the top of the neck, but we worked on it a bit and it's reasonably accurate now. But yeah, I do use it and it's got a great tone."

While so many guitar and bass players of the fifties and sixties were influenced by other players in their choice of instrument, Paul has another story...

"To tell you the truth it was because I was left-handed. Every guitar I ever used had to be right-handed, because back then they didn't make special left-handers, so I used to have to turn them upside down. But the violin shape was symmetrical so it didn't look quite as stupid as some of the others did - for instance when their cutaways were on the up-side."

While most of the guitarists who have commented on their Hofners in terms of their playability have admitted that they fell short in one or two departments, the same does not seem to be true of McCartney's Violin bass...

"I love the fact that it's not heavy," enthuses Paul. "I noticed a clip of me in the 'Let It Be' film, playing on the roof, and you know you play differently when the instrument itself isn't heavy. You're tempted to play more melodic riffs and more, kind of, guitar parts, really. So I think it's great. I think its tone, for a little lightweight bass, is incredible, because it really sounds like a string bass sometimes. So I like it a lot. Its main problem is the inaccuracy in the tuning when you get up the neck a bit."

The small, lightweight bass that Paul describes must surely have needed work carried out if the instrument was frequently in use - refrets, etc...

"We've done a little bit of work - more on the bridge and stuff, because of the tuning problems - but not a lot. I think it's still basically original; I think it's still the same instrument!"

Companies like Rickenbacker made great use of the fact that their instruments were used and endorsed by the The Beatles. Was there a similar relationship for Paul with Hofner - free gear, for instance?

"There was none whatsoever, actually, outside of the fact that I publicised their bass for them. But I never did a deal with them. I decided not to get into any of that stuff, so I didn't really know them much. Didn't get any free gear either, I don't think. They might have given me a bass early on, but as far as I can remember there was not much of a relationship at all. I just admired their bass."

In 1968 a deluxe model Beatle bass was introduced. The 'Super Beatle' boasted a flamed maple back and rims, a spruce top finished in clear lacquer, elaborate bindings, pearl inlay and gold hardware. This limited edition G500/1 model also featured a unique mix and bass boost circuit. A guitar version was introduced the same year, but was dropped from the line not long afterwards.

So how does Paul McCartney assess the influence of Hofner guitars and basses over the music made by The Beatles and the other beat groups of the sixties?

'You know, I think that Hofner were some of the first people with any decent instruments; not only the violin-shaped bass but their guitars as well. Obviously my big influence was the bass, but a few of the lads had the guitars and, even though they weren't quite as good as, say, Fender or Gibson instruments, they had a great sound. I think a lot of people liked that distinctive sound."

Alvin Lee

Alvin Lee's performance with the group Ten Years After stands out as one of the memorable highlights of 1969's famous Woodstock festival. His speedy rendition of 'Going Home' confirmed his reputation as one of the fastest guitarists around. Lee's trademark guitar, both then and now, is his Cherry red Gibson ES335, with its distinctive and unmistakable Ban The Bomb sticker. But although Lee owns a Hofner guitar now, a Senator, he did not learn on a Hofner or even own one as a teenager...

"My first guitar was a Zenith, whatever that was. But I bought a Hofner Senator some fifteen years ago, and I do occasionally use it for recording. It's got a very country sound about it; actually it sounds incredibly like a Stratocaster. But the action on mine's set so low that the strings are almost buzzing on the frets, so you get that kind of 'ring'."

Alvin was never terribly smitten with Hofner guitars, if the truth be told. "Of course I remember them being a big name. But the mystique to me was all about American guitars, which probably made Hofners sound like a cheap alternative, although I'm sure they weren't. I mean, the Committee was a pretty cracking job, now that I think about it. But I remember Tommy Steele had one and he got voted best guitarist of the year in one magazine, and I don't think he could even play!"

While legions of guitarists tell of the days when they'd stand and gaze longingly at the Hofners in their local guitar shop window, unfortunately Alvin had no such loving memories...

"Not a Hofner, no. But I did travel twenty miles to see a band that allegedly had a real Fender! And they actually had two - a Strat and a bass."

Albert Lee

Although an Englishman, Albert Lee is regarded by many as the best country guitarist in the world. So highly regarded is he that James Burton asked Albert to take his place in Emmylou Harris's Hot Band when Burton left to rejoin Elvis Presley; he is called on for endless sessions, where his fast and fiery playing style is unmistakable; Albert was Eric Clapton's sideman for five years on the road and he now plays with Don and Phil Everly wherever they tour in the world. On top of this, Lee tours the UK and Europe every year with Hogan's Heroes, a band comprised of Albert's friends, all of them English session musicians.

"I think it was the Christmas of '58 when my folks bought me a Hofner President," remembers Albert. "They got it via the Exchange & Mart; it cost either £23 or £25 and it had one pickup screwed onto the end of the fingerboard, so it was really an acoustic with a pickup added. It came in a canvas bag, as I recall."

Albert didn't keep his President for long, because he soon realised he wasn't able to do the things he wanted to do on it. "No, the things by Cliff Gallup, of Gene Vincent's Blue Caps, and the stuff that Buddy Holly played, needed a solid guitar, without dodgy pickups and things like that," he laughs. "So I traded that in for a Grazioso, which was the original name for Futurama guitars. I think most of the people who started around the same time as I did went through the same phase; I know Tony Sheridan had one and George Harrison had one too. The Grazioso was a cheap alternative in the late fifties, early sixties, to a Fender, when Fenders first started coming into the country."

"And that President was the only Hofner I ever owned, and of course we all wish we had our original guitars, but I traded my one in so it's long gone now. I always thought Hofners were very well made, although the necks were a bit chunky - a bit tree-trunk-like for me - and from what I can remember they were fairly narrow all the way down the fingerboard, making the strings fairly close together."

"But I remember seeing the Committees in the early days... they were beautiful to look at. It was sad, though, because later on in the sixties you'd walk into Selmer's in Charing Cross road to ogle the Gibsons, and there was a whole wall of Hofners that they used to call the 'Hofner Graveyard'; dozens of Hofners that no-one wanted. But I'd love to own one of those old Committees now, just so I could look at it."

Hilary Giltrap

Midge Ure

MidgeUre's first guitar was not actually a Hofner. It was a Watkins Rapier, given to him by a friend's father. "He had two of them," recalls Midge, "a 22 and a 33, and he gave me the 33 because I was more interested in music than he was." Midge's first amplifier came the same way: "This guy owned an electrical shop, and people would put amps in for repair and never collect them, so he'd repair them and then six months later he'd give them to us. I was about eleven or twelve and it was like I'd died and gone to heaven. I had a real electric guitar and an amplifier that I could plug it into."

Like many guitarists of the day, Midge wanted but never actually acquired a Hofner. So, as a member of the successful band Slik, he set about fulfilling this childhood dream, eventually stumbling across his Hofner in London's Camden Market. "It was in 1976 that I found it hiding behind a pile of junk on a stall," he reminisces, "looking a bit lost and forlorn. It cost me the princely sum of thirty pounds; I saw it and thought, 'Thirty pounds, that's got to be mine.'"

Midge has actually used his Hofner, too. 'Just after the big hit record that I had with the band Slik, we did a series of concerts and in the show we did a 1940s Cole Porter / Irving Berlin kind of thing and I used it on that. It actually sounded quite good."

Midge's Hofner was unfortunately never particularly playable, with a crack on the back of the neck which was there when he bought the guitar. "In fact I actually bought it more for the aesthetics than the playability," he willingly admits, "and I've probably mimed a few things on Top Of The Pops with it."

"But a Hofner was definitely something to aspire to. I mean, the nearest I ever got to a guitar in those days was the competitions on the back of Kelloggs' cornflake packets, to try and win a Burns Bison. And you used to cut those things out and stick them up on your wall, like all kids do. The other thing was to order the Bell catalogue from the back of one of the music papers, and that had millions of photographs of Hofner guitars. That was the nearest I ever got to a Hofner in those days."

Although he didn't play many Hofners as a teenager, Midge's main memory of them concerns their rather high actions: "It's possibly because of the fixed wooden bridge," he says; "you could raise it, but the problem was you couldn't get it down low enough to get any kind of action out of the thing. But I suppose in those days it didn't really matter much, because I wasn't playing any lead - I never went anywhere near the top of the neck, it was all chords down the bottom."

In Ure's circle of musician friends there were other Hofner guitars. "One of the guys had a Verithin, which lived up to its name because it was very thin - about an inch deep, or something. And quite a few Hofner basses were doing the rounds at that point, as well. Hofners were very good, accessible, affordable guitars when you were starting out, because everyone wanted a Gibson SG or a Les Paul; everyone wanted a solid guitar and Hofners, being semi-acoustics, weren't particularly fashionable. Everyone wanted the solidbody beast of a thing!"

Hilary Giltrap

"So at that time the Hofner became the poor relation, although of course it didn't really deserve the tag. In the fifties it was a sought after guitar, a nice instrument to have, and it was those instruments that sparked me off. I mean, seeing Tommy Steele in the movies with this great big, fat-bodied guitar - which he very rarely actually strummed - was my first image of people with guitars; I remember thinking, 'Yes, that's what I want.'"

Midge has an interesting story concerning a Hofner electric 12-string; his 'mythical' guitar, as he calls it. "I was in a bootmakers in Glasgow, in a very dodgy area - it was around the time when platform boots were in vogue and we couldn't buy them for love nor money. But I'd heard this guy made them, and being the groovy character that I was I went along to try and get some made. And I met some guy in there, a very dodgy character in a very dodgy area, and he said, 'Are you a musician?' - my long hair and platform boots probably gave me away - so I said, 'Yes'. And he said, 'I've got a guitar for sale, I'll bring it in.' And he came back about five minutes later with this Hofner semi-acoustic 12-string, with two pickups and a single cutaway. I'd never seen one like it, but I bought it - I don't know where he got it from and I wasn't particularly interested at the time - and it was a bit of a bargain. I used it on stage in the group that was the forerunner for Slik, a band called Salvation. I was the guitarist and the singer and we played cover versions like Rod Stewart's 'You Wear It Well.''

"I actually used this thing for about a year before I decided to trade it up for something else. I remember getting nineteen pounds for the guitar in McCormack's in Glasgow. I wish I'd kept it now; it was such a nice thing."

Ritchie Blackmore

Ritchie's Club 50 with Bigsby.

Of all the great British rock guitarists who emerged in the sixties, one of the finest was Deep Purple's Ritchie Blackmore. Blackmore took private lessons from the great Jim Sullivan, and the two soon formed a mutual appreciation society, Sullivan citing Blackmore as his best ever pupil and Blackmore rating Sullivan as simply 'one of the most accomplished guitar players on this earth'. Big Jim had played a Hofner and traded it for a semi-solid ES345 and Ritchie was to do likewise.

"The Hofner was my second guitar," he recalls. "I got it when I was fourteen or fifteen; it was a blonde Club 50 which I eventually had to sell to buy my Gibson 335. I often wonder what happened to it, because you don't see them around very often now. The Hofner Club line were wonderful guitars, although I wouldn't play them much on stage because they didn't cut through that well. But like everyone else I remember looking through the

magazines at fourteen and thinking how wonderful they all were."

Again, like so many of his contemporaries Blackmore would stand for hours, gazing in shop windows at guitars... "That's what it was all about then; these days you just go out and buy what you want and it doesn't have the same impact. On Saturday mornings I used to go up to Selmer's, look at the guitars in the window, stay for an hour and then go home. Having said that, I actually got the Club 50 from Jim Marshall's shop in Ealing."

Whilst it's plain that some guitarists merely tolerated their Hofners as 'the best they could get', others adored them, including Blackmore..."I loved mine," he grins. "I remember playing my first date with it, down at Feltham Town hall, and then loads of other places - Southall Community Centre and places like that.."

Ritchie kept his Club until he was sixteen, when the offer to join the infamous Screaming Lord Sutch's band forced him to use it as a down payment on his Gibson ES335.

"But the Club wasn't exactly cheap when my parents bought it for me; I think it cost thirty-two guineas (£33.60), and that was a lot of money in those days."

Guitarists are great tinkerers, and Ritchie Blackmore was no exception, fitting a Bigsby tremolo unit to his Club 50.

"But it was the one that screws directly onto the soundboard," he confesses, "not the one that attaches where it's more solid, on the bottom rim. I was certainly taking a chance there! I did the same thing with my Gibson, and that was definitely the screw-on one on the soundboard, but on the 335 it's solid wood underneath there, not like the Hofner, which was hollow."

Blackmore agrees with other guitarists that, compared to Gibsons and Fenders, which could handle the high volumes suddenly demanded by bands in the sixties, Hofners were often let down by their pickups.

"They were a bit too boomy and that made them feed back on the bass end. But I loved the neck on mine, and the actual craftmanship of the guitar was incredible."

Although he regrets the loss of his Club 50 as a piece of personal history, Ritchie has never replaced it. But were he ever to do so, the guitar would almost certainly not be used on stage... "I'd probably use it in the studio, though, and in fact I do need to get one because I also like the Gretsch guitar, but I never got around to getting one of those because I'd never use it on stage. Actually I'd love to play my Club 50 again, just to see how it felt. It had a rather bulky neck - narrowish, but bulky at the back- but I was used to that. Now all guitars have very thin necks."

And what British guitarist from the sixties doesn't remember Cathedral strings? Hank Marvin certainly does and so does Ritchie.

'Yeah, they'd be very twangy for about ten days and then they'd go dead!"

And along with so many of his contemporaries Blackmore's first amplifier was a Watkins Dominator - although Ritchie's blew up on its first outing...

"It blew up on the first number: Curtains opened, amp blew up, curtains closed! So I took the whole thing back to Selmer's the following Saturday, on the underground. They gave me another one which I took back to the station, all the way back to Hounslow West and went back to my house, which was about three miles further, hobbling with this Dominator. Well, the same thing happened; we played somewhere else and it blew up on the first number! I couldn't believe it! After about the third one the guy in the shop said, 'Bring your guitar in next time and we'll figure out why you keep blowing this amplifier up.'"

"So a week later I went in, we plugged my guitar in, I started playing and it blew up. I got through about five Dominator amps. In the end he gave me another amp and I said, 'Can I try it out first?' He said, 'No, just get out of the shop!' He couldn't stand me any more. And I took that one and it never broke down. But it's funny how he wouldn't let me try it in the shop." Ritchie reckons that the guitarists of today have things a bit too easy. Guitars and amps are cheap, and by and large they're well made and reliable. Even beginners can usually find an amp to use with their first electric guitar...

"With my first guitar, which was a Framus, I put three pickups on it myself and I used to have to plug it into the radio, because I didn't have a guitar amp. They don't have to do things like that any more."

"But I remember, I played at a Christmas concert at school and I was having trouble with the pickups - I couldn't figure out why the guitar wasn't working through the radio. So after about half an hour I plugged the guitar straight into the mains because I was so confused at what was happening. And I fused the lights in the whole of the school! I grabbed my amplifier - my wireless - and ran!"

Justin Hayward

Although Moody Blues guitarist Justin Hayward didn't start out on a Hofner, he did have one, a Club 60, bought while he was still at school in the very early sixties. "I'd like to see that guitar now," says Justin, "because now I know all about intonation and fixing things and making sure the action is exactly right. So I'm curious; I was never sure how good they were, because it's a guitar that everybody goes through on the road to something else. I suppose I had it for about a year before I traded it in for the big, three-pickup Harmony H75."

Hayward really wanted a Gibson ES335, the guitar he eventually became best known for. He also knew that the Hofner Club was shaped rather like a famous Gibson... "But it wasn't until later that I discovered this was the Les Paul."

Hayward bought his Club 60 in Swindon in Wiltshire, although he can't be positive about its cost. "It was probably about thirty pounds." And although many players found the pickups lacking in clout Justin felt his were just fine. "I thought it sounded great! There was a little plate with a knob at either end and then some little switches in the middle. It had two black pickups; I don't think there were any pole pieces or anything; I think they were just set underneath two black pieces of plastic."

"Actually the pickup were very woolly, now I come to think about it. Of course, back then you never got up to the volume that you play now, so I wouldn't know how it would respond to really high volume. But I loved it as a guitar because there was something about it that was very friendly and very warm - always such a lovely feel. And it was the first real, proper guitar that I had."

"Before that I had a Japanese Broadway guitar and a couple of other things that were real Mickey Mouse, probably Eastern European. And I had a Rosetti Lucky 7 for a while, a white one, same as everybody..."

The music that Justin Hayward played on his blonde Club 60 was mainly Buddy Holly covers. "Buddy Holly was Number One for me and so I knew everything that he and any of the combinations of his backing people had ever done. I knew all of those solos and everything. I wasn't in a group with a singer out front; I was in a group that was just three guitars, or two guitars and drums. And so it was Buddy Holly, with a bit of Curtis Mayfield thrown in; funny combination, but that was about it."

Like the majority of his peers Justin loved The Shadows, although his taste gradually started to change: "I'd got close to the Shadows' sound with a Futurama, but I never could afford a Strat and I was actually never a Strat person. It was always a Gibson that I was after and I was always looking for semi acoustics."

Along with his various Gibson ES335s Hayward is also well known for playing a sunburst B-45 Gibson 12-string acoustic, which he still uses. 'The Gibson is really good if you're going to hit it," says Justin, "but for any kind of delicacy I have a Martin, with silk and steel strings, which is wonderful."

"But I love that Gibson 12-string and I leave it in a big C tuning for a song called 'Questions', and every time I get it out and hit those chords it sounds absolutely brilliant. And when I play it in front of other people they always go, 'Cor, that's that sound, isn't it?"' Justin is in agreement with Joe Brown on Hofner's influence on the sixties and British rock'n'roll in general. "Yes, it was the same for me as for everybody else: it was everybody's proper, real guitar; real craftsman made. I used to love the headstock. I loved the way the word Hofner

was done on the head. I used to wake up in the morning and just look at it. I'd prop it by the bed at an angle, so that when I woke up I could look straight at it.."

Hayward believes he would use his Club 60 today, if he still had it. "I think I would, because Hofners had a particular feel about them; they just felt very comfortable and warm, and for a certain kind of record they were a very soothing kind of guitar. But that was also their drawback - they were built for comfort, like a Rover car, but there was really no aggression about them. Some of them were a bit too much like jazz guitars, but I never wanted one of those great big fat ones."

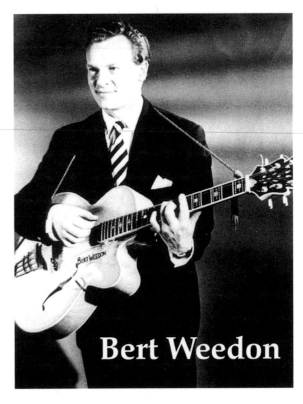

Bert Weedon

One of the stalwarts of the British fifties and sixties music scene, Bert Weedon's tutor 'Play In A Day' proved to be the foundation on which many great careers were laid. Not only was Weedon a regular radio guitarist, but he was also featured prominently on Childrens' television, giving playing lessons on programmes like '5 O'clock Club'. Weedon also had several chart hits, including 'Guitar Boogie Shuffle', the first guitar record to get into the British hit parade, back in 1959.

Bert Weedon's association with Hofner began when Ben Davis and Lew Lewis, saxophonist and trombonist in the famous Jack Hylton band, opened a music shop in London's Charing Cross Road. The shop was Selmer's and soon became THE place to go to buy guitars.

One day, Ben Davis called Bert and told him about a new guitar: 'We're calling it a Committee' said Davis, 'and I'd like you to play it and tell me what's right with it and what's wrong with it'. Weedon continues the story:

"Then he said, 'I'd like you to have this guitar and play it for us.' I was doing a lot of

radio work and occasional TV shows, so I started to play the Hofner Committee. And when I looked at it I thought it was such a beautiful guitar. And I still think they're the most beautiful looking guitars because the inlays and the artwork is so beautifully done."

"Then they brought out a thinner model, the Golden Hofner, and then the Verithin. And as they brought each model out, Ben Davis said to me, 'Would you play this one and bring the old one back', and like a fool I gave them all back!"

Weedon maintains that it was his influence which prompted other players to choose Hofners. "Hofner was delighted that, through my exposure, Paul McCartney and John Lennon started to play Hofners. I was doing quite a lot at the time, and papers like Melody Maker and New Musical Express used to advertise 'Bert Weedon plays Hofner' and all the up-and-coming guitarists bought them because of that."

Eventually, dissatisfied with the power of the Hofner pickups, Weedon spoke to Davis: "I said to Ben, you know, the American guitars are starting to come over and their pickups are far superior'. So Ben got in touch with Hofner and told him to improve the pickups. Ben used to write to them and say, 'We've got to get a better sound', or 'Bert Weedon says the action could be better and the neck should be a little thinner', because it was rather chunky in the early days. And gradually they introduced a thinner neck and the action and pickups got better. Eventually though they couldn't compete with the Americans and I told Ben he must do something or he would lose sales."

"Gradually the Guild guitars started coming over and I thought, 'Well, I can't wait any longer', so I switched to Guild and they were very co-operative." I had a Starfire and they asked me to help them design a Bert Weedon model. I was very thrilled about that, because I think that was the first American guitar ever named after a British guitar player."

On Weedon's regular slot on '5 O'Clock Club' he would often demonstrate innovations, such as the Bigsby tremolo arm...

"I got Selmer's to put a Bigsby on a Hofner for me, because they were also the agents for Bigsby tremolo arms and DeArmond pickups. But on '5 O'Clock Club' I would often try and introduce a pickup or a vibrato arm or an echo chamber. I suppose I was an innovator in those days; now I don't really know what's happening with all the electronic gimmicks and things. But I think my use of the Bigsby influenced the Hofner factory to fit them as standard on some models. The tremolo arm at that time was a very important development in guitar playing, a very innovative and exciting sound."

At the time of writing Bert Weedon is contemplating the fitting of some better pickups on his blonde Hofner, figuring the guitar is well worth the trouble: "They're such lovely looking instruments," he reiterates. "The workers who did the inlays had centuries of historical background in that kind of work; it was a place where carving and inlay work were traditional. In America it was a relatively new thing, but in Germany, Austria and Italy they had been doing mandolins and other instruments for

years. I don't think, even today, there are guitars that equal it."

Today, Hofner maintain that to build a Golden Hofner would cost well over £2,000; when they were introduced they retailed for well under a hundred.

"Well," reasons Bert, "a four hour recording session used to pay three pounds. These days I think it's about a hundred and twenty, so if you work it out it's about forty times; forty times, say, seventy-five pounds is three thousand pounds. But, you know, they were expensive back then, and jolly hard to get, because it was a period of austerity, when you couldn't really get suits and even food. So when Selmer's started importing Hofners it was marvellous."

"I was doing an awful lot of broadcasting then, and when lads like Tommy Steele and Marty Wilde were growing up they used to listen to me, and when they got well known they nearly always said, 'Could we have Bert Weedon playing?' And because I played a Hofner a lot of them played Hofners - or held Hofners."

"So in the fifties and sixties they were THE guitar, although they gradually lost out to the Americans. But had they kept pace with their pickups, I'm sure they'd still be the top guitar, because the action is beautiful, and you hardly ever see a Hofner with a warped neck. That company did a marvellous job and were very special in the history of the guitar."

Joe Brown

Hilary Giltrap

"I've got a picture somewhere of me with a Club 50" says singer, TV personality and all-round good guy Joe Brown. "Those guitars were the only real, decent guitars available in this country around the late fifties, and we were all very impressed with the mother-of-pearl inlays on them. What was the big, flash one? The Committee, that's right. But they were also good guitars in that they had their own sound."

"Of course I went on to Gibsons after that, and I went through various others, including Emile Grimshaw, a bloke in North London who used to make guitars. I had a little short-scale white one, with thousands of knobs on it. But before that I had the Hofner, and although I've always thought they weren't as good as Gibsons, really, they did have their own tone. Unfortunately it was that American rock sound that we were all after, and Hofners didn't have that sound. But in the old days there was no British rock sound, and I think the Hofners had a great deal to do with giving us a sound that was peculiar to British rock'n'roll."

"I don't know much about them except the Club was the one to get; and I had one of them! I don't know what happened to it. I probably bought it at Selmer's in Charing Cross Road, because that's where we all went for our guitars in those days. Then Selmer's became Gibson agents, and that's why so many of us changed over to Gibson."

Joe, top left, with his Club 50.

Joe's memory is vague when it comes to the price he paid for his Club, but he has a theory: "Was the price anything to do with the numbers on them, like Gibson? For instance, the ES335 was $335 and the J-200 was $200. Whether the Club 40 was forty quid or not, I don't know, but it sounds about right. And the Club 60 could have been about sixty quid.."

"They were all the same size, those Club models. There was the Club 40 and Club 50, and the Club 60 was the top of the range with all the inlays. Most of the bands had them, of course, and they were a reasonable guitar, a good guitar in fact. But then everyone heard Chuck Berry with his Gibson and Eddie Cochran with his Gretsch, and we all went on to the American guitars after that."

The semi-acoustic nature of most Hofner guitars ensured that when players changed allegiance to, for instance Gibson, they very often chose semi's .Joe Brown was no exception, opting for a Gibson ES335.

"As a matter of fact I went bloody mad round about the middle seventies. I decided I was fed up with my 335 and so I went out and bought a Les Paul solid, and I just couldn't get on with it at all! But I'd sold my 335 and I've never had a guitar like it since. I used to get a feeling about it - I could actually feel the thing when I played it. Sometimes you pick up a guitar and you think, 'This is great', and you can get 20 guitars the same make but they don't feel right, and you know it's not just the fingerboard or the neck or the pickups, it's everything about it."

"Anyway, I sold the thing to Selmer's, and Roy Wood bought it. And Roy's got it in a flightcase in his garage and Jeff Lynn and George Harrison and all these people have been 'phoning him up, saying, 'Go on, do us a favour Woody, sell it back to Joe'. But Woody won't part with it. So I said to him 'Come on mate, I want it back; I'll buy it off you', but he said to me, 'I'll leave it to you in my will'. So I warned him to check his milk in the morning, just in case I slip something into it!" Anyway, I've got all the lads to keep mentioning my guitar to him. So who knows..."

Roy Wood

"The first guitar I ever had was a Hofner Colorama," says Roy Wood, the talented songwriter, multi-instrumentalist, original guitarist in The Move and co-founder of the Electric Light Orchestra. "It was Cherry Red with a sort of a gold stripe round the edge. It had a black scratchplate, a single cutaway and it had a single black, plastic pickup. And it didn't have a tremolo arm," he states, with some dismay.

"But in those days I wanted to play like Hank Marvin, so I had a tremolo put on it. It wasn't like a Bigsby, it looked more like the type you find on Fender Stratocasters."

"The next guitar I had was a Hofner V3, which was a sort of orange-coloured one with a black scratchplate and chrome pickups. And that did have a tremolo on it, which was more like the Bigsby. I got that in the early sixties.

Being from the generation that came after Joe Brown and Bert Weedon, Roy was one of the many young guitarists whose prime influence was the music of The Shadows, and the guitar playing of Hank Marvin.

"I started buying Shadows' records quite a bit before I started playing," says Wood. "And groups like The Ventures and the Crew Cats; I was very keen on all the instrumental stuff, because a friend of mine was a big Ted (Teddy Boy) and he liked Cliff and the Shadows and he used to buy all their records. So I got interested through listening to the guitar solos."

Wood had seen pictures of The Shads and had seen or heard Hank Marvin mentioning the Fender Stratocaster. And that, Roy reckons, was what started him off.

"Also, in those days, if anybody in the area had got a guitar, you knew about it. They were famous! So, through another friend of mine, I got friendly with a group of lads who used to play in the Church Hall. They were much older than me - I was about fifteen or sixteen and they were all early twenties. They were all at work and I was still at school. But I was always very keen on music; I used to play the drums and a chromatic harmonica down at the local Working Men's Club, with a piano player. So I got into it quite quickly and I learned to play the solos quite quickly, too, even though at that time I wasn't so good on the chords. So I got the job with them as lead guitarist."

"Guitars were obviously a lot cheaper in those days; a Fender Strat cost, I think, a hundred and eighty-nine guineas. But my first Hofner guitar was about forty or fifty quid, and the second one was probably about eighty odd pounds, which is probably the equivalent of about eight hundred today."

"The trouble was, compared to the American guitars the necks were awful on them, to be honest. For some reason mine didn't take long to warp. With my first guitar it was probably due to the fact that I hadn't got a solid case; I just had it in one of those plastic jobs. And the action was always difficult; it was quite high, and neither me nor my mates knew what to do about it. I mean, I wouldn't have dared to take the bridge off and mess around with it. And I seem to remember that on the V3 the neck was a bit fat, and I haven't got very big hands so I always found the action a bit of a drag."

Roy Wood traded up from his Hofner V3, and here his Shadows influence comes to the fore...

"I got a pink Fender Strat. I've still got it today and it's a really good one. I'd started work then and I was saving up my money and my Mum and Dad helped me get it on hire purchase. I was actually playing in a group properly then and my Dad said, 'Well, you're taking it seriously so we'll see what we can do'. And there it was! It was from Jack Woodroff's in Hill Street in Birmingham; it was hanging on a wall in a polythene bag and they wouldn't let anybody touch it. And one of the great things I remember about that was, when I got it back home and opened the case, the smell of the paint, that celluloid sort of smell, it used to attach itself to the case so it always smelled really new. It was great!"

"Of the most available guitars then, the most popular solid guitars for beginners were the Hofner, the Futurama or the Burns. Of the three I preferred the Hofner- certainly the V3 - although the original Colorama I had was terrible."

"The first amp I had was called Supersound; it was a little green thing, a pile of rubbish. Then I got some advice off somebody and I bought one of those Linear amps, the one with the metal cage over the top. It was a valve amp. I bought some speakers and my Dad made a cabinet for them. In fact he made cabinets for everybody in the band and we all had them made much bigger than they needed to be, just to look flash! After that I got a Bird amplifier, with reverb on it. And I remember we used to play 'Telstar', by the Tornados, and at the beginning of the song I used to kick the amp to make the reverb sort of explode, just for the effect."

"The funny thing about that Linear amp was that it was actually not a guitar amp, it was more of an electronic buff's type of amp. Anyway, we used to play this school hall and I got this portable television aerial, one of the old V-shaped ones, and I used to put it on top of my amp and just shove the plug in a hole in the back of the speaker cabinet, not actually attached to anything. And I used to have all the young kids coming up and asking what it was. And I used to say, 'Oh, it's remote control for the guitar!'"

Dave Gilmour

When Dave Gilmour joined Pink Floyd in the late sixties it was originally to augment the guitar work of Floyd's founder and frontman Syd Barrett. However, Barrett's ever-stranger behaviour led to his leaving the group and Dave staying on. The line-up of Gilmour, Roger Waters (bass, vocals) Rick Wright (keyboards, vocals) and Nick Mason (drums) was to become one of the most successful in rock history, their album 'Dark Side of the Moon' still included among the best sellers of all time.

Gilmour's guitar work is thoughtful, melodic and always appropriate for the occasion. He is chosen by artists such as Paul McCartney and Kate Bush to guest on their records and is generally regarded as one of today's finest electric guitarists. Gilmour is most commonly associated with Fender Stratocaster and Telecaster guitars, but one of his earliest and most fondly remembered was a Hofner Club 60. "The Club 60 wasn't actually the first guitar I had, but it was the first one I finally settled with after two or three others. The one I had before the Club was a Burns Trisonic, a pretty weird thing which I didn't like very much. Then I saw this guitar in my local music shop. It actually had the neck broken off and I said to the bloke in the shop, 'What's happening to that guitar?' and he said 'It's in for repair'. I told him I'd like it, and I got it for thirty quid, including the Bigsby tremolo."

Dave bought his Club from Ken Stevens' music shop in Cambridge, around 1963, and kept it until he acquired his first Fender, a Telecaster. "I actually persuaded my parents to give me a Telecaster for my 21st Birthday. I did hang on to the Hofner for bit, but then I owed somebody some money, so I gave them the guitar to sell and keep the money. So that was the end of that, really. It was a great shame, because it really was a nice example. I've got one again now, which I bought a few years ago, but it's just not as nice as the original one I had."

Gilmour's Club 60 was one of the early, 'black pickup' models – "I didn't like the

humbuckers" he says – and his replacement guitar is very similar – "except that the neck's a little fatter."

Has Dave ever used his Club 60 in anger? "I don't think I've ever used it on record, although I do get it out and have a go on it once in a while. But my original one was my main guitar for three or four years, from when I was seventeen up until I was twenty-one. So I used that and really liked it. In fact, when I was in Spain a guy with a Les Paul Junior liked the sound of it so much that he offered to swap, but I said 'No!'"

Gilmour's Cambridge band was called Jokers Wild, and the group's repertoire included mainly rhythm and blues tunes. Dave bought his replacement Club 60 around the turn of the eighties, for purely nostalgic reasons. So how does he think they compare with the guitars of today?

"Well, a really nice one is a fine guitar. They had a really good sound and I found those single coil pickups were quite good, quite pokey, but the pots they used and the electronics let them down. In fact you could have made them a lot better by working on things like the electrics, which is what I would do if I was using one today."

Some of Dave's contemporaries have said their Hofners were overly warm and woolly sounding, but Dave disagrees. "I don't know, I think mine was quite Telecaster-y, quite sharp. You could certainly make quite a good rock'n'roll sound with it – at least that's what I found."

Martin Taylor

Without doubt one of the world's finest guitarists, Martin Taylor can captivate an audience with a phenomenal technique which combines bass figures, chordal accompaniment and melody lines – all at the same time! Add to this a depth of feeling and an improvisational ability second to none, and you'll appreciate why Martin sometimes replaces Herb Ellis in the 'Great Guitars' alongside jazz legends Barney Kessel and Charlie Byrd.

Taylor's early guitar influences were Django Reinhardt (Martin's father sat him down and said, 'Listen to this, son, this is the greatest guitar player in the world'), Eddie Lang, Karl Kress, Dick McDonough and George Van Epps. But Martin says his style really developed from listening to the way pianists – the great Art Tatum in particular – combined the elements of bass, rhythm and melody into their playing.

Currently a Yamaha user – Martin plays a guitar co-designed by himself and ex-Yamaha guitar technician and designer Martyn Booth – he does, however, have fond memories of a day in 1958 when the postman arrived with two packages . . .

"The packages were for my dad; one was a guitar and one was an amplifier. The amp was a Watkins Westminster and the guitar was a Hofner President. I can still remember the thrill when my dad opened the case – a hard case

with plush velvet lining – and this beautiful, shining Hofner gleemed out at us. And I can still remember, vividly, the smell of the guitar. I think it was that that really put me on to playing – once that guitar case was opened I was hooked.

"When I was very young, my brother and sister would be at school and my dad was at work (me being the youngest member of the family) and my mum used to let me play Dad's guitar, although she didn't tell him because she thought he wouldn't like me messing about with his brand new instrument. But I used to sit on a chair – I was very small then, only about three or four – and she used to put the guitar on my knee so I could play. So that was the start of it for me, and obviously a Hofner is the guitar that did it, as it did for so many guitarists in the British Isles who grew up around the fifties and sixties. The Hofner was THE guitar for us.

"There was always this kind of dream for guitarists in Europe to get an American guitar, a Gibson or a Fender, but I don't think a lot of guitar players realised just how good the Hofners were. But there was this sort of mystique attached to owning an American guitar, but now, of course, a lot of guitar players understand what qualities the Hofner had. The guitars are becoming, not just collectable, but people are remembering how playable they were.

"Hofner's archtop guitars have a very distinct sound. I sit and play my dad's every so often and I really like playing it because of this particular sound. It doesn't sound like an L5 or a Super 400, but it has a sound, and a feel, which is all its own. You can't really compare it, or say one's better than the other; it would be a matter of taste, your choice. The guitar that we've got, the President, has actually got a very warm, full sound. Even on the top strings the sound is very thick, and I like that guitar very much.

"When my dad retired, just a couple of years ago, I replaced his Hofner President – because he sold his when he took up the double bass – with one as near as I could get to the original, so we've got one in the house again."

A Personal Collection

Gordon Giltrap's collection of Hofner guitars,
showing a small sample of the many
beautifully crafted instruments that helped to
shape the world of modern guitar playing.

Golden
Hofner

1960
S/N 27

Golden Hofner

This is very similar to the 1961 Golden Hofner also featured in this book except the clear scratchplate is missing and it has a Micromatic bridge as opposed to the regular Hofner bridge with the fixed fretwire intonation saddles. This one has been used a lot more as a gigging guitar. It is also doubtful that the control knobs are original. This guitar came to me with its rather battered original case.

Razorwood
1980s
Model S7/12

Razorwood

Imported into this country by Barretts of Manchester the rather unusual shaped Razorwood came in 6- and 12-string versions and featured a solid mahogany body, Schaller machineheads, active electronics and coil tap. This guitar has one of the best actions I have ever played on a 12-string.

Detail of tailpiece and controls

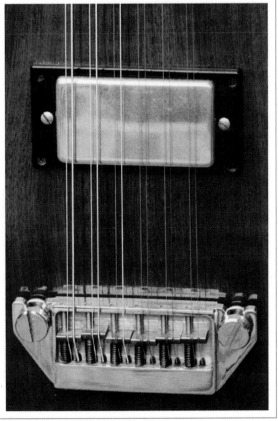

Detail of Pickups

463/S/E3
1965

463/S/E3

Unusual three pickup model made for the European market only, acquired in Denmark and bought by me from a shop in Bristol. It has a handsome bowed back and multi-coloured wood binding front and back. Sides and back are made from mahogany.

Convenient pickup switches

Details of unusual three pickups and elegant tailpiece

Colorama
1960
S/N 213

Colorama 444

I was given this guitar complete with its original case and strap (and the guarantee featured in the memorabilia section of the book). The Egmond tremolo arm, which is not original, is a rather Heath Robinson affair in as much as it raises the strings to achieve a tremolo effect, defying all the laws of playability and action. Instant bottleneck!

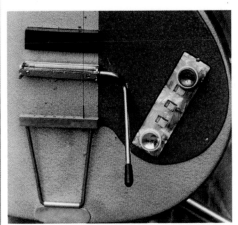

Detail of tailpiece and controls

Detail of pickups

President
1958
S/N 3458

President

The staggered tailpiece on this model is rather unusual with the sixth string retainer being the same length as the fifth.

Note the lack of truss rod cover, showing the guitar to have been made before 1960.

Congress
1958
SN 7376

Congress

This was very much a budget model and retailed at fourteen guineas when it first came on to the market. This was the model that Hank Marvin started out with. The condition of this particular instrument is immaculate. It is virtually unplayed. The style of the headstock changed with later models, otherwise the instrument remained basically the same. After my interview with Hank he kindly signed this guitar for me.

Detail of tailpiece and signature

Committee
1957
S/N 2518

Committee

I had always regretted
selling my first Committee,
bought from Musical
Exchanges in Birmingham
and featured on the sleeve
of my album 'Gordon
Giltrap – Guitarist' so when
I saw this one in the
window of a music shop in
Wallasey the day following
a concert I couldn't resist it
and blew the bulk of my fee
on it. It is all original and is
in superb condition. Bert
Weedon kindly signed this
one for me.

**Committee
Thin Line**
1957
S/N 1026

Committee
Thin Line

The birdseye maple is particularly beautiful on this model and my thanks go to its previous owner Steve Rowley, and also to Bob Bowman for pointing me in the direction of this wonderful guitar.

Detail of the pickups

**Committee
Sunburst**
1958
S/N 2752

Committee Sunburst

The pickup surrounds on this early example are made of wood with Trepholite capping. It seems as though the pickups varied from model to model, the most common from this period being the plastic cover type. A piece was missing from the bass of the scratchplate so I modified the shape slightly following the straight line of the pickup side. This guitar appealed to me so much that I traded in five guitars for it!

Detail of bridge and pickups

Tailpiece and bridge detail

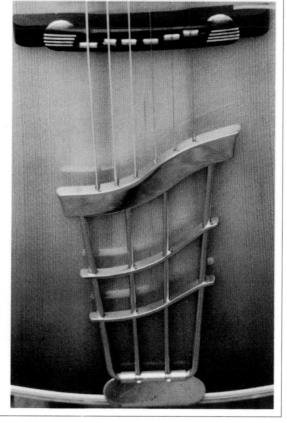

Golden Hofner
1961
S/N 57

Golden Hofner

This guitar was featured in Paul Day and Tony Bacon's 'The Ultimate Guitar Book' and is a superb example of this model. The Golden Hofner was top of the range and when one looks at the quality of the woods used and the detailed inlay, multi-purfling and gold plated, engraved hardware one can see why. This quite rare guitar has a remarkable tone when played acoustically.

Detail of the tailpiece

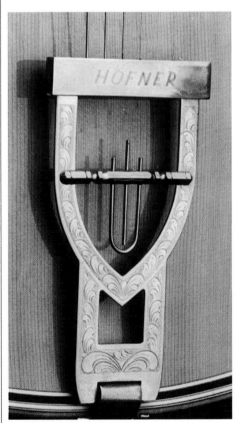

Detail of pickups and scratchplate.

Note the superb edge and inlay detail

**Golden
Thin Line**
1960
S/N 16

Golden Thin Line

All original with its case, complete with 'gold' scratchplate. This one has Art Deco style pickups. The Golden Hofner was made for export only in very limited numbers and was a very expensive guitar for its time, retailing at 95 guineas. If Hofner were to make one today it would cost 7,000 DM – approximately £2,800.

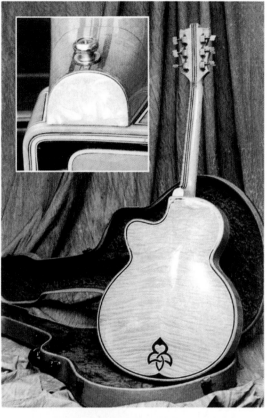

Detail of the machineheads.

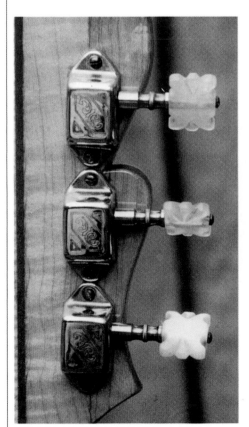

Distinctive motif with heel inlay shown inset.

Pickup detail with gold supported scratchplate.

Club 60

The Hofner Club Series was quite a favourite amongst players, with its Les Paul styling and warm sound. The Club 60 was the top of the range and featured flick action controls and a lavishly inlaid ebony fingerboard. John Lennon and Paul McCartney were two of the many players who favoured Club guitars in their early days.

Note the striking flamed maple, typical of the Club 60.

Detail of tailpiece and controls

Detail of pickups

Club 60
Sunburst
1961
S/N 1063

Club 60 Sunburst

The mini Bigsby on this particular guitar may not have been fitted as standard and could have been added later. The diamond logo pickups were used from 1961 to 1963. Again note the beautiful bookmatched maple veneer.

**Violin
Bass**

Hofner
Verithin

Galaxy
176

My first Hofner was a Verithin and was similar to the early sixties model pictured above with the Bigsby tremolo unit. The Verithin proved to be quite popular with its semi-acoustic body resembling the Gibson 335. Mine came complete with a hard rectangular shaped case and it took me forever, it seemed, to pay off the HP!

The Galaxy was very similar in styling to the Fender Strat and its obvious appeal was the colour, shape and numerous tone variations. It was the all singing, all dancing model with three pickups, slider controls, string damper and tremolo unit.

Opposite is one of two violin basses owned by Paul McCartney. Paul used this guitar for many years in concert and on numerous Beatles albums. This is the famous one with the Beatles set list taped to the side of the guitar.

Rebirth of a Hofner

Gordon Giltrap's 1962 Committee
Thin Line SN 1280

It was during a tour with jazz guitarist Martin Taylor that I met Bert Wapplington. Bert had heard I was collecting Hofners and offered to give me an old instrument of his. He told me that it was in a poor state of repair, but I didn't realise just how poor. Bert said he would bring it along to the next convenient concert and sure enough, he did - in a carrier bag! The neck was completely adrift from the body; all the frets, along with most of the inlays, had dropped out; any remaining bits were in a separate bag. The guitar also had the remains of a mouse nest inside the body! The pickups, machineheads and controls were completely ruined, and the arm from the original Bigsby was missing. Also, much of the decorative body binding had gone. Bert informed me that this was how it came to him – I can only assume that it

had been left in a garden shed for years. What a way to treat such a beautiful instrument.

I took it to my local repair man, Alan Exley of R.M.I. Music Company, Redditch, who rose to the challenge of rebuilding it. It was decided to replace everything apart from the neck and body. Various bits of body binding were obtained from Hofner and the hardware is mainly Japanese, including Yamaha machineheads, pickups and bridge; the tailpiece, I believe, is American. The missing inlays had to be cut by hand and Alan said, whilst refretting the neck, that the ebony was the hardest he had ever come across.

As you can see by the photographs, the Committee was in a very sorry state at the start, and because the body was damaged

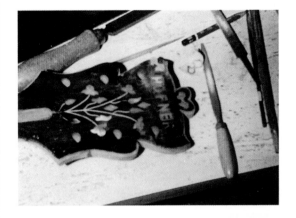

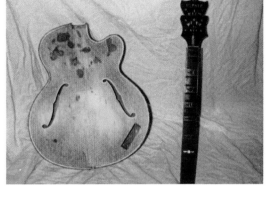

A few photographs showing just how extensive the damage was.

in parts, Alan decided to finish it in a slight sunburst.

I think the end result is marvellous – truly a labour of love and a tribute to Alan's time, patience and skill in restoring the guitar to its former glory.

Repaire Alan Exley with the finished guitar.

Gordon Giltrap

Gordon Giltrap

MEMORABILIA

Remember the days before decimal currency? That's when you could buy things for pounds, shillings, pence, guineas and farthings, and when you could "Play in a Day" for about 6/-.

The following pages show some early Hofners featured in the old Selmer catalogues along with ads for guitar cases, add-on pickups and such like. Note the changing faces of the various models through the years. See Paul Day's chapter on dating Hofners for details.

Guarantee

This is to Certify that *Colorama Guitar 2 p/ups*

Serial No. *213* is hereby Guaranteed to the original purchaser for the term of

FIVE YEARS

Should it, within that time, show any defect caused by unsatisfactory workmanship, we undertake to put same defect right provided that:

1. All repairs of any description to the instrument are carried out by us or our approved agents only.
2. The instrument has not been replated, engraved, or any metal deposited thereon except by us.
3. Any defect is caused by poor material and/or faulty workmanship but not through ordinary attention or wear and tear.
4. This guarantee and receipt is produced at the time of complaint.
5. Guarantee has been registered with us within 7 days of purchase.
6. Whilst replacements under guarantee are supplied free, a labour charge will be payable for fitting same.

CARE O...

DRYING
Acid laden mo.......... the wind
instruments. The ....soned wood may
crack if water is alle........p into the bore, tenons
or joints. Whilst t......fect on metal is not so pro-
nounced, perspiration or breath moisture can cause
corrosion.
For wood wind instruments the extra expense of a
fitted case is well worth while. The fitted case rules
out the human element and the player is forced, on
the Clarinet for example, to detach the mouthpiece
and barrel in addition to separating the centre joint.
All tenons should be thoroughly dried after use and
the bore swabbed with a Selmer Clarinet Mop.

GREASING
Cork joints on wood wind instruments and tuning
slides on bass instruments should be treated every few
weeks with Selmerlube, a refined instrument grease
with a pre-determined melting point.

OILING
The bore of wood wind instruments can be pro-
tected by the application of Selmer Bore Oil. Apply
both inside and outside before use and repeat the
treatment twice a week for the first month and at
weekly intervals thereafter.
The springs and bearing rods on saxophone and
clarinet should be lightly dressed every few weeks
with Selmer Key Oil.

GUITARS
Guitars should not be strung above or below pitch,
as this causes undue strain on the instrument, use a
set of pitch pipes or piano to check the pitch. When
not in use the guitar should be kept in a room of even
temperature.

Selmer

114-116 CHARING CROSS RD., LONDON, W.C.2

TO PURCHASER

...tect your interests as the owner of this
...u to fill in, detach and post the attached
. The Guarantee is not valid unless it is
...ithin 7 days from date of purchase.

...not apply to natural substances used in the
...ent, e.g., wood used in clarinets, oboes,
...:.; pads and springs in similar woodwind
...Both saliva and perspiration have a corrosive
...ing to the individual. In consequence, though
...workmanship or materials, Selmer cannot
...ng.

Selmer

CROSS ROAD, LONDON, W.C.2

Guarantee

A few of Hofner's prime endorsers of the time.

Britain's 'top six' guitarists have contributed to the specification of this fine guitar. The Committee Model has a 17½ inch top, hand carved from old straight grained pine. Domed back and sides are veneered in birds eye maple with handsome mother o'pearl finish purfling. Spliced steel reinforced neck faced with rosewood cambered fingerboard inlaid with mother o'pearl on marquetry panels. The magnificent head has a frondose outline and mother o'pearl marquetry. Fittings are of a standard which measure up to the guitar workmanship. Screw cog, steel worm, plated and engraved single machines; best quality lyre style tailpiece; ebony adjustable bridge, floating transparent celluloid fingerplate.

No. 369 Committee Model, blonde 48 gns.

No. 368 Committee Model, brunette 48 gns.

(Page 4)

Committee

ACOUSTIC/ELECTRIC MODELS
INCORPORATING

 CONSOLE

with the new "flick action" change!

VOLUME 2	RHYTHM	BASS ON	TREBLE ON	VOLUME 1
	SOLO			

"New Line" DOUBLE PLATE CONSOLE

The "New Line" console is now incorporated in all Hofner acoustic/electric and electric guitars. Now you can make a "quarter beat" flick change from rhythm to solo— "edgy" or round tone colours in a flash. Single or double plate consoles according to model.

COMMITTEE ELECTRIC

The same specification as the famous COMMITTEE acoustic with the addition of two built-in Hofner high sensitivity pick-ups and "New Line" double console with two volume controls, rhythm/solo switch plus bass and treble controls.

No. 395 Committee electric
blonde   63 gns.
No. 396 Committee electric
brunette   63 gns.
No. T395 Committee blonde
Thin model   63 gns.
No. T396 Committee brunette
Thin model   63 gns.

Committee ELECTRIC

5

NEW THIN
ELECTRIC GUITARS

To meet the increased demand for Electric Guitars several exciting new instruments have been added to this year's range. The new "thin" style guitars are available for the first time in this country in the famous Hofner range. All the Hofner electric guitars will now be obtainable in the new "thin" form, thus enabling the discerning player to have all the advantages of the latest design coupled with the craftsmanship synonymous with the name Hofner. The thin models have been developed as electric guitars. They are lighter and more compact than the conventional guitars, but have a "big" guitar sound.

Available with either single or double "FLICK ACTION" console controls.

When ordering thin models from the Hofner range add the prefix T to the standard model catalogue number—the price remains the same.

Golden Hofner
electric guitar

Built to the specification of guitar specialists, the Golden Hofner is unmatched in elegance and unequalled in tone.

Frets are of nickel silver, and machined heads are totally enclosed.

For complete specification see Golden Hofner Acoustic, page 2.

The Golden Hofner incorporates the "New Line" Flick Action console exclusive to all Hofner Electric Guitars. This enables quick changes from rhythm to solo playing and change of tone colours by the "flick" of a switch.

Cat. No. 523 .. .. 95 gns.
Thin model
Cat. No. T523 .. .. 95 gns.

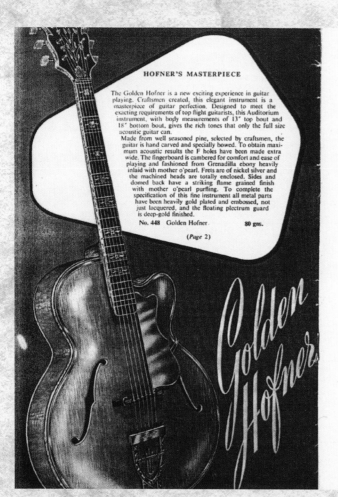

HOFNER'S MASTERPIECE

The Golden Hofner is a new exciting experience in guitar playing. Craftsmen created, this elegant instrument is a masterpiece of guitar perfection. Designed to meet the exacting requirements of top flight guitarists, this Auditorium instrument, with body measurements of 13" top bout and 18" bottom bout, gives the rich tones that only the full size acoustic guitar can.

Made from well seasoned pine, selected by craftsmen, the guitar is hand carved and specially bowed. To obtain maximum acoustic results the F holes have been made extra wide. The fingerboard is cambered for comfort and ease of playing and fashioned from Grenadilla ebony heavily inlaid with mother o'pearl. Frets are of nickel silver and the machined heads are totally enclosed. Sides and domed back have a striking flame grained finish with mother o'pearl purfling. To complete the specification of this fine instrument all metal parts have been heavily gold plated and embossed, not just lacquered, and the floating plectrum guard is deep-gold finished.

No. 448   Golden Hofner.   80 gns.

(Page 2)

Golden Hofner

GUITAR PICK-UPS

HIGH IMPEDANCE

No. 320

HOFNER POPULAR

Reduction in the price of this new pick-up has been effected purely by simplifying the design of the Standard Model No. 352. The sensitivity is unimpaired but the pole pieces are not individually adjustable. The casing is plated like the Standard Model and the Popular Model comes complete with lead and jack plug.

No. 320 Popular model without adjustable pole pieces .. £2.3.6

No 352

HOFNER CELLO TYPE

Jack Llewellyn and Roy Plummer are two of the many top-line guitarists who use the new Hofner magnetic pick-up. Models 352 and 349 have screw-slot adjustable pole pieces for individual string response adjustment. New model with integral volume control has improved graduated linear response. Pick-up can be affixed to any cello guitar by inserting small screws in the adjustable brackets.

No. 352 Standard Model £3.2.6

No. 349 With volume control .. £4.7.6

HOFNER ROUND HOLE TYPE

The Hofner magnetic pick-up is now available for round sound hole guitars. This new model is exactly the same integral design and will give the same high standard of reproduction as the established cello type. The new fitting enables the pick-up to be secured on the edge of the sound hole without damage to the soundboard by affixing plates above and below the wood.

No. 345

No. 345 Standard Model £3.2.6

No. 346 With volume control .. £4.7.6

HOFNER DOUBLE PICKGUARD UNIT

This revolutionary new pick-up enables two separate heads to be moved to any position between the bridge and fingerboard by simple sliding action. Tonal colours are subsequently infinitely variable, giving complete tonal perfection. A separate magnet for each string on both pick-up heads banishes tuning problems. Control is by dual volume control knob and three "new line" flick switches. With this combination many novel effects are obtainable such as banjo and mandolin tones. The unit is in one piece and is finished in mirror chrome. Easily fitted to any guitar by slotting into the bridge.

No. 506. 12 gns.

SUPER SENSITIVE
Forte Guitar Pick-up

A compact guitar unit in attractive gilt finish, suitable for use with all high impedance amplifiers. An easy fitting is obtained by means of maleable metal bar to grip both sides of the neck. Impedance 4,500 ohms. This unit will meet the exacting requirements of the connoisseur.

No. 525. £3.17.6

HOFNER TAILPIECE CONTROL PICK-UP

Here at last is the complete conversion set for the player who wishes to use his existing guitar for electric work. The standard Hofner pick-up is connected by a covered cable to a tone and volume control unit affixed to a special tailpiece. Fitted with "rhythm and solo switch". Both units are clear of the soundboard and do not affect the guitar's acoustic properties. The connecting lead is insulated and permanently connected to both units and in consequence the **tailpiece control unit cannot be supplied separately**. Both units heavily plated.

No. 322 Tailpiece Control Unit £6.5.0

NEW MODEL PICK GUARD PICK-UP UNIT

A new self-contained unit for cello guitar. Converts your standard acoustic to a top grade electric model. Easily fitted as the sensitive magnetic pick-up is built in to the chrome-plated fingerplate which is fitted with tone and volume controls.

No. 319 .. .. £4.10.0

HOFNER ELECTRIC
BASS GUITAR

THE electric bass guitar has opened up a new field for fretted instrument players. The instrument widely used in America is tuned like a bass, identical with the third, fourth, fifth and sixth strings of the guitar. The provision of frets ensures accuracy of intonation and means that the guitarist can play this new instrument right away. Fitted with the "New Line" double plate console. Ease of portability is another advantage of this new instrument which enables the guitarist to double his income.

SPECIFICATION

Domed top and back with double purfling: 30" scale. Guitar type adjustable bridge. Tortoiseshell finish fingerplate. Trapeze style tailpiece. White purfled F-holes. Two sensitive pick-up units with tone and volume controls for each. Heavy screw machines. Laminated neck with thick fingerboard and pearl position dots. Body width 17¼". Overall length 45½". Complete in rigid domed shaped case, felt lined.

No. 328. Hofner electric bass guitar, blonde .. .. .. 48 gns.

No. 333. Hofner electric bass guitar, brunette .. .. 48 gns.

COLORAMA

SOLID ELECTRIC GUITARS

These new Hofner guitars are of the "solid type". Carved from selected timbers their completely solid construction renders them virtually indestructible. The built-in electrical unit provides the big sound and tone variety required today. Light and compact in design, these professional models are available in colour combinations with attractive finishes. Either single or double New Line flick action controls are fitted.

Double Pick-up Model
No. 444   22 gns.

Single Pick-up Model
No. 443   18 gns.

Club 60

WITH THE "NEW LINE"

flick action console.

A smart newcomer to the famous "Club" range, with a slick "stagey" appearance. Designed on "semi-acoustic" principles, with fully vaulted back, the Club 60 is fitted with the "New Line" flick action change console, two Hofner high sensitivity pick-ups, adjustable bridge for height and tuning compensation. Smart mother o' pearl embellishments on head and fingerboard, carefully embedded nickel-silver frets.

No. 425 Club 60 Blonde 40 gns.
No. 442 Club 60 Brunette 40 gns.

A new model designed specifically for electrical work. The body is built on "semi-acoustic" principles which give the tone a round character not found in solid instruments. The shape and fretting of the neck is designed to facilitate modern rapid chord and single string passages. Bridge adjustable for height and tuning compensation. Nickel silver frets, screw cog machines and reinforced plated tailpiece. One built-in Hofner Super-unit. Single plate New Line console. Complete with amplifier lead.

No. 389 Club 40. Blonde and brunette models available. 27 gns.

A similar model to the Club 40 but fitted with two Hofner Super-units—each with tone and volume controls, and on/off switches. The "feel" of the specially designed necks must be experienced; the section is cut down to minimum width and strings are set close to the rosewood fingerboard in which buzz-free frets are carefully bedded down over their entire length. The body is gracefully cut away to give easy control of the extreme top register. The two units offer a wide range of tonal effects. Double plate New Line console. Complete with amplifier lead.

No. 390 Club 50. Blonde and brunette models available. 33 gns.

11

NEW HOFNER CLUB 70

Designed specially to meet a popular demand for a guitar of this styling, the Club 70 is a superb newcomer to the famous Hofner range, built on semi-acoustic principles to provide a character of tone not normally found in solid body guitars. The body shape and fretting of the neck facilitate the easy playing of intricate single-string passages and rapid chording. It is fitted with two Hofner high-efficiency bar pick-ups (see page 2), adjustable bridge for height and tuning compensation, heavy duty machine heads and separate volume and tone controls for each pick-up. Body dimensions: 17⅛" x 12⅞" x 2⅛".

No. 5108. Club 70 .. .. .. 52 gns.
No. 5909. Rich felt-lined shaped
          case £14 0 0

Cases, see page 34

4

DE ARMOND PICK-UP

5

NEW HOFNER AMBASSADOR

The Ambassador is the outcome of Hofner's many successful years of guitar making. Only experience and craftsmanship can produce such quality at an economical price. All the well-proven and exclusive Hofner features—"Slenda-nek" cambered rosewood fingerboard, adjustable truss-rod, Micro-matic bridge for fine tuning. Now fitted with two Hofner high-efficiency bar pick-ups (see page 2). Rich golden sunburst finish. All this adds up to one of the most exciting models ever to leave the Hofner workshops. Body dimensions: 20¼" x 15½" x 1¾".

No. 5126. Brunette .. .. 80 gns.
No. 5906. Rich felt-lined case £13 10 0

AMBASSADOR WITH DE ARMOND PICK-UP

The Hofner Ambassador De-Luxe is now also available. Fitted with two of the world-famous American De Armond pick-ups. These double-pole models are finely designed to the most exacting standards, giving you the correct frequency response on each string—plus higher sensitivity than ever before.

These fantastic pick-ups, plus fine Hofner craftsmanship, give you an all-round sound comparable to any other guitar on the market. Proved to be popular! What more could any player ask for with these two great names linked together. Hofner and De Armond.

No. 51261. Brunette, with De
           Armond pick-up 86 gns.
No. 5906. Rich felt-lined case £13 10 0

Cases, see page 34

PRESIDENT ELECTRIC

DOUBLE PLATE CONSOLE

PRESIDENT ELECTRIC

Same specification as the President Acoustic Model, with the addition of two Hofner high sensitivity pick-ups, and a "New Line" DOUBLE PLATE CONSOLE

No. 385	President, blonde	..	..	44 gns.
No. 386	President, brunette	..	..	44 gns.
No. 385T President, blonde thin model				44 gns.
No. 386T President, brunette thin model				44 gns.

SENATOR ELECTRIC

Same specification as the Senator Acoustic model, and fitted with a "New Line" SINGLE PLATE CONSOLE.

No. 387	Senator, blonde	..	27 gns.
No. 388	Senator, brunette	..	27 gns.
No. 387T Senator, blonde, thin			27 gns.
No. 388T Senator, brunette, thin			27 gns.

SINGLE PLATE CONSOLE

8

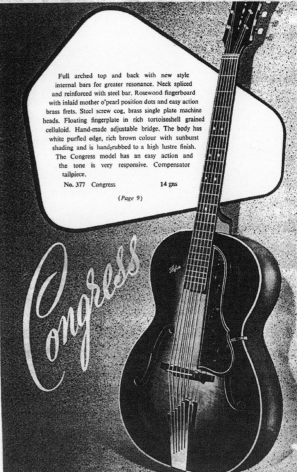

Full arched top and back with new style internal bars for greater resonance. Neck spliced and reinforced with steel bar. Rosewood fingerboard with inlaid mother o'pearl position dots and easy action brass frets. Floating fingerplate in rich tortoiseshell grained celluloid. Hand-made adjustable bridge. The body has white purfled edge, rich brown colour with sunburst shading and is hand-rubbed to a high lustre finish. The Congress model has an easy action and the tone is very responsive. Compensator tailpiece.

No. 377   Congress   14 gns

(Page 9)

Congress

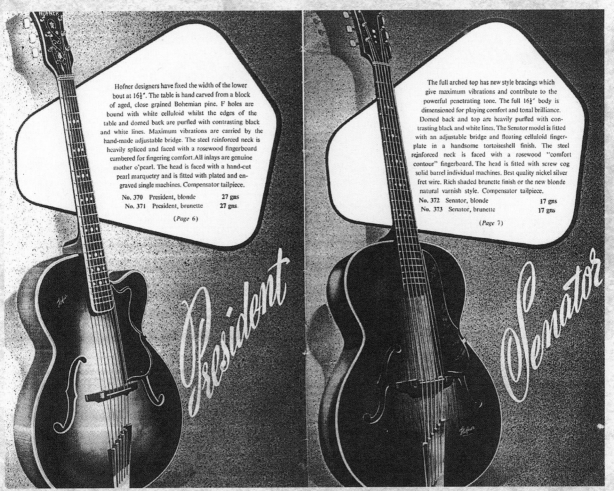

Hofner designers have fixed the width of the lower bout at 16¼". The table is hand carved from a block of aged, close grained Bohemian pine. F holes are bound with white celluloid whilst the edges of the table and domed back are purfled with contrasting black and white lines. Maximum vibrations are carried by the hand-made adjustable bridge. The steel reinforced neck is heavily spliced and faced with a rosewood fingerboard cambered for fingering comfort. All inlays are genuine mother o'pearl. The head is faced with a hand-cut pearl marquetry and is fitted with plated and engraved single machines. Compensator tailpiece.

| No. 370 | President, blonde | 27 gns. |
| No. 371 | President, brunette | 27 gns. |

(Page 6)

President

The full arched top has new style bracings which give maximum vibrations and contribute to the powerful penetrating tone. The full 16¼" body is dimensioned for playing comfort and tonal brilliance. Domed back and top are heavily purfled with contrasting black and white lines. The Senator model is fitted with an adjustable bridge and floating celluloid fingerplate in a handsome tortoiseshell finish. The steel reinforced neck is faced with a rosewood "comfort contour" fingerboard. The head is fitted with screw cog solid barrel individual machines. Best quality nickel silver fret wire. Rich shaded brunette finish or the new blonde natural varnish style. Compensator tailpiece.

| No. 372 | Senator, blonde | 17 gns |
| No. 373 | Senator, brunette | 17 gns |

(Page 7)

Senator

Selmer

GUITARS

and STRINGS

THE BIRMINGHAM BAND INSTRUMENT COMPANY.
Musical Instruments Specialists,
213, Lichfield Road, Aston, Birmingham, 6.

NEW *Hofner* FEATURES

THIN LINE MODELS

New Slenda-nek

NEW ADJUSTABLE INTERNAL TRUSS ROD

"FLICK ACTION" CONSOLE CONTROLS

VOLUME 2	RHYTHM	BASS ON	TREBLE ON	VOLUME 1
		SOLO		

Fitted to the President Electric, Senator Electric, Club and Colorama Guitars.

No. 687   £1 1 0

Now, as always, Hofner lead the field in guitar design. Of primary importance is the wonderful Hofner New "SLENDA-NEK" now standard on all models; these necks are the thinnest ever. But a thin neck must also be strong, and to this end the "Slendaneks" have new type internal metal truss rods making them the strongest ever. The truss rod is adjustable by a simple screw mechanism in the head which makes it possible to take up any play in the neck and is the final answer to warping. All electric models incorporate the Hofner "SUPER RESPONSE" PICK-UPS. The unique arrangement of the six pole pieces completely eliminates the over-powering second string tendency found in normal pick-ups. This new Hofner design has been fully adjusted by experts before fitting to the guitar, avoiding tiresome adjustment by the player. New mechanism enables you to raise or lower the pick-up accurately and quickly by two single screws; and the lower pick-up has been reversed. These great advances in pick-up design give you correct frequency response on each string plus a higher sensitivity than ever before. This pick-up is exclusively fitted to Hofner guitars and is now available as a separate item. See page 20.

Don't forget that all electric 'cello guitars in the Hofner range are also available in the THIN LINE. When ordering these models from the Hofner range, add the prefix "T" to the standard model catalogue number—the price remains the same.

Some Hofner guitars are fitted with slick, CALIBRATED ROTARY CONTROLS. The calibration enables the player to accurately pre-set the separate tone and volume controls.

The MICRO-MATIC BRIDGE makes it possible to tune your guitar to perfect accuracy on each individual string, at the bridge. It permits precise adjustment for intonation and each saddle can be reversed individually for full range tuning. Easily adjusted for fast, low action. Fitted as standard to the following guitars: Committee Electric and Acoustic, President Electric and Acoustic.

2

NEW *Committee* Electric

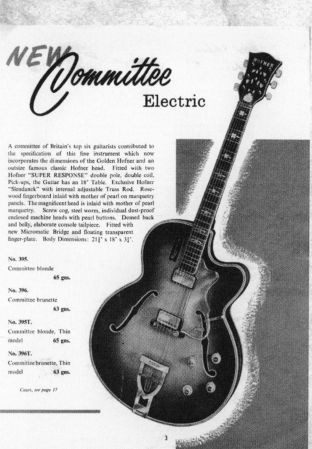

A committee of Britain's top six guitarists contributed to the specification of this fine instrument which now incorporates the dimensions of the Golden Hofner and an outsize famous classic Hofner head. Fitted with two Hofner "SUPER RESPONSE" double pole, double coil, Pick-ups, the Guitar has an 18" Table. Exclusive Hofner "Slendaneck" with internal adjustable Truss Rod. Rosewood fingerboard inlaid with mother of pearl on marquetry panels. The magnificent head is inlaid with mother of pearl marquetry. Screw cog, steel worm, individual dust-proof enclosed machine heads with pearl buttons. Domed back and belly, elaborate console tailpiece. Fitted with new Micromatic Bridge and floating transparent finger-plate. Body Dimensions: 21¼" x 18" x 3¼".

No. 395.
Committee blonde   65 gns.

No. 396.
Committee brunette   63 gns.

No. 395T.
Committee blonde, Thin model   65 gns.

No. 396T.
Committee brunette, Thin model   63 gns.

Cases, see page 17

3

Verithin by Hofner

Run your fingers over the frets of this thinnest of all guitars (see inset) and you'll feel the superb proportions of the wonderful "Slendanek" on this elegant instrument. Only craftsmen like Hofner—steeped in years of traditional skill—could combine this with the modern functional lines of this magnificent instrument. Its fine acoustic tone is transmitted through two Hofner "SUPER RESPONSE" double pole pick-ups to give unequalled treble performance. Acoustic tone is virtually unimpaired by the slender design.

Beautifully styled for the Professional Player, cherry red finish with cambered rosewood fingerboard, and nickel-silver frets. Head and neck inlaid with mother of pearl marquetry. Individual machine heads. Fitted with new Micromatic Bridge. Body Dimensions: 20¼" x 16½" x 1¼".

No. 299   ..   ..   52 gns.

No. 494 with Bigsby Unit   ..   64 gns.

Cases, see page 17

The 'Bigsby' True Vibrato Unit can be supplied fitted to any Hofner and Gibson Electric Acoustic guitar, as illustrated, at a supplementary charge of 12 gns.

4

NEW PRESIDENT
Electric

Fitted with two Hofner "SUPER RESPONSE" double pole pick-ups. Controlled by double-plate "FLICK ACTION" console control. F holes are bound whilst the edges of the table and domed back are purfled with contrasting black and white lines Exclusive Hofner "Slendanek," the strongest, thinnest Guitar neck ever, with new internal adjustable Truss Rod. Single machines, heavily engraved, fitted to head faced with hand-cut mother of pearl marquetry. Best quality lyre style tailpiece. **Fitted with new Micromatic Bridge.**

Body Dimensions : 20¼" x 16" x 3¼".

No. 385.
President, blonde .. .. **48 gns.**

No. 386.
President, brunette .. **46 gns.**

No. 385T.
President, blonde, thin model .. .. **48 gns.**

No. 386T.
President, brunette, thin model .. .. **46 gns.**

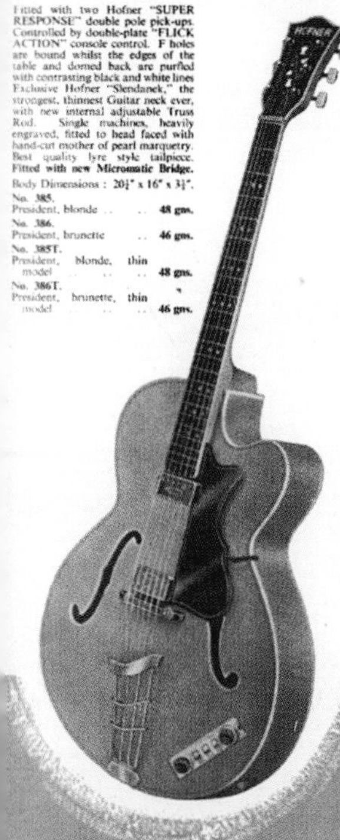

SENATOR
Electric

Fitted with one "SUPER RESPONSE" double pole pick-up. Controlled by single-plate "FLICK ACTION" console control. Exclusive Hofner "Slendanek" gives you faster playing action and the new internal metal Truss Rod allows adjustment of the neck. Powerful tone, and 20½" x 16½" x 3" body dimensions. Contoured for playing comfort. Rosewood cambered fingerboard. Single solid barrel machine head. Nickel-silver fret. Compensator tailpiece.

No. 387.
Senator, blonde .. .. **28 gns.**

No. 388.
Senator, brunette .. **27 gns.**

No. 387T.
Senator, blonde, thin .. **28 gns.**

No. 388T.
Senator, brunette, thin .. **27 gns.**

Cases, see page 17

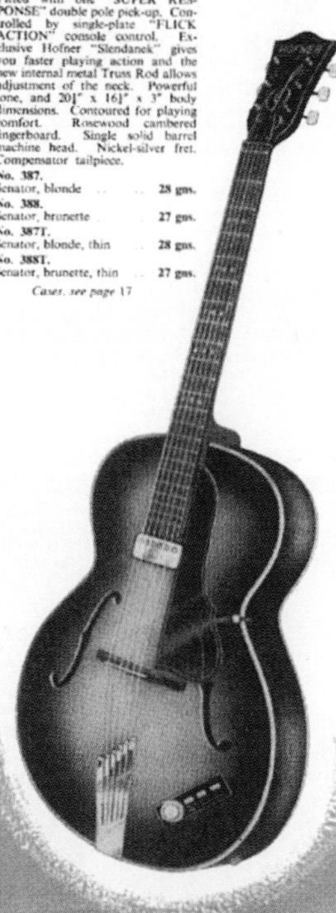

CLUB 60

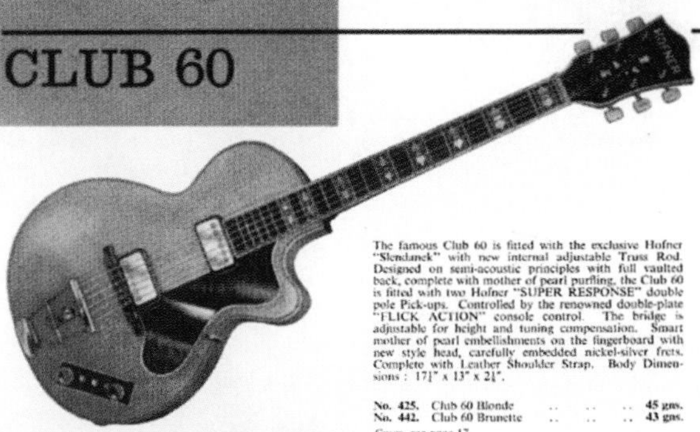

The famous Club 60 is fitted with the exclusive Hofner "Slendanek" with new internal adjustable Truss Rod. Designed on semi-acoustic principles with full vaulted back, complete with mother of pearl purfling, the Club 60 is fitted with two Hofner "SUPER RESPONSE" double pole Pick-ups. Controlled by the renowned double-plate "FLICK ACTION" console control. The bridge is adjustable for height and tuning compensation. Smart mother of pearl embellishments on the fingerboard with new style head, carefully embedded nickel-silver frets. Complete with Leather Shoulder Strap. Body Dimensions : 17¼" x 13" x 2¼".

No. 425. Club 60 Blonde .. .. .. **45 gns.**
No. 442. Club 60 Brunette .. .. .. **43 gns.**

Cases, see page 17.

CLUB 50

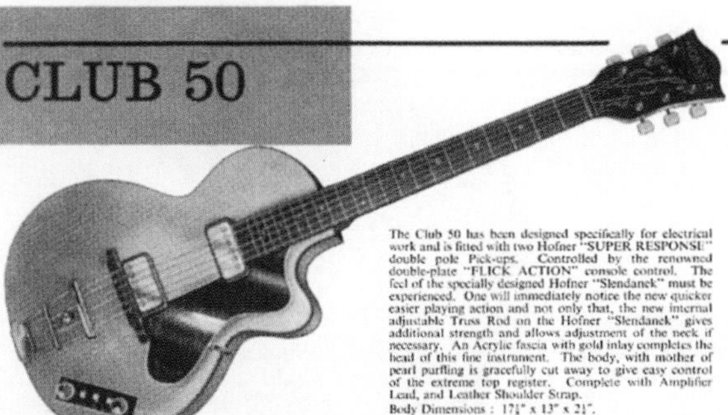

The Club 50 has been designed specifically for electrical work and is fitted with two Hofner "SUPER RESPONSE" double pole Pick-ups. Controlled by the renowned double-plate "FLICK ACTION" console control. The feel of the specially designed Hofner "Slendanek" must be experienced. One will immediately notice the new quicker easier playing action and not only that, the new internal adjustable Truss Rod on the Hofner "Slendanek" gives additional strength and allows adjustment of the neck if necessary. An Acrylic fascia with gold inlay completes the head of this fine instrument. The body, with mother of pearl purfling is gracefully cut away to give easy control of the extreme top register. Complete with Amplifier Lead, and Leather Shoulder Strap.

Body Dimensions : 17¼" x 13" x 2¼".

No. 390. Club 50. Blonde .. .. .. **36 gns.**
No. 536. Club 50. Brunette .. .. .. **35 gns.**

CLUB 40

A similar model to the Club 50 but fitted with one Hofner "SUPER RESPONSE" double-pole pick-up. Complete with Amplifier Lead and Shoulder Strap.

Body Dimensions : 17¼" x 13" x 2¼".

No. 389. Club 40. Blonde .. .. .. **30 gns.**
No. 535. Club 40. Brunette .. .. .. **29 gns.**

Cases, see page 17.

Hofner Super SOLIDS

with Built-in Tremolo

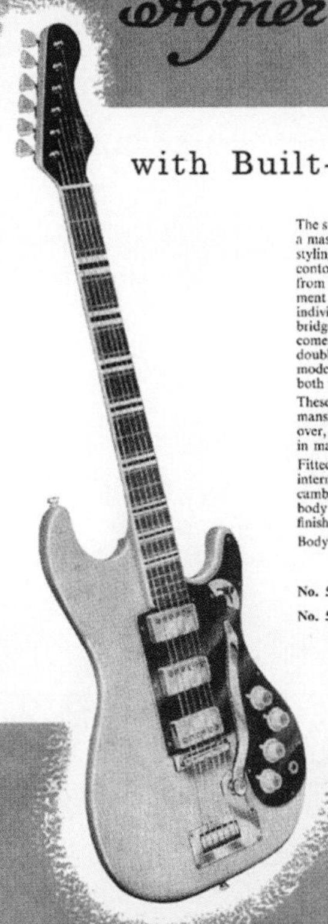

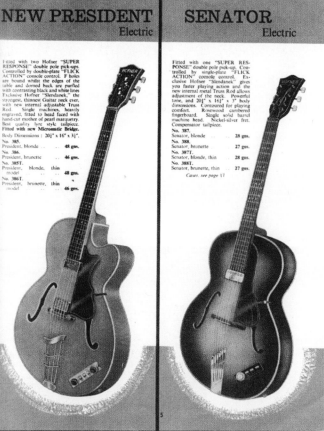

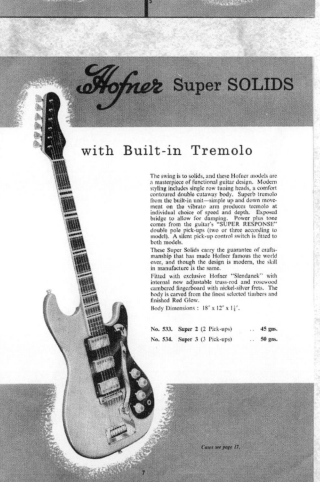

The swing is to solids, and these Hofner models are a masterpiece of functional guitar design. Modern styling includes single row tuning heads, a comfort contoured double cutaway body. Superb tremolo from the built-in unit—simple up and down movement on the vibrato arm produces tremolo at individual choice of speed and depth. Exposed bridge to allow for damping. Power plus tone comes from the guitar's "SUPER RESPONSE" double pole pick-ups (two or three according to model). A silent pick-up control switch is fitted to both models.

These Super Solids carry the guarantee of craftsmanship that has made Hofner famous the world over, and though the design is modern, the skill in manufacture is the same.

Fitted with exclusive Hofner "Slendanek" with internal new adjustable truss-rod and rosewood cambered fingerboard with nickel-silver frets. The body is carved from the finest selected timbers and finished Red Glow.

Body Dimensions : 18" x 12" x 1¼".

No. 533. Super 2 (2 Pick-ups) .. **45 gns.**

No. 534. Super 3 (3 Pick-ups) .. **50 gns.**

Cases see page 17.

Colorama SOLIDS

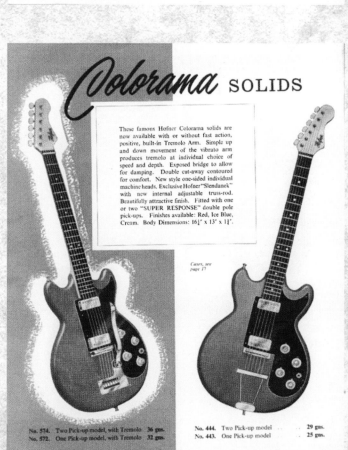

These famous Hofner Colorama solids are now available with or without fast action, positive, built-in Tremolo Arm. Simple up and down movement of the vibrato arm produces tremolo at individual choice of speed and depth. Exposed bridge to allow for damping. Double cut-away contoured for comfort. New style one-sided individual machine heads, Exclusive Hofner "Slendanek" with new internal adjustable truss-rod. Beautifully attractive finish. Fitted with one or two "SUPER RESPONSE" double pole pick-ups. Finishes available: Red, Ice Blue, Cream. Body Dimensions: 16¼" x 13" x 1¼".

Cases, see page 17

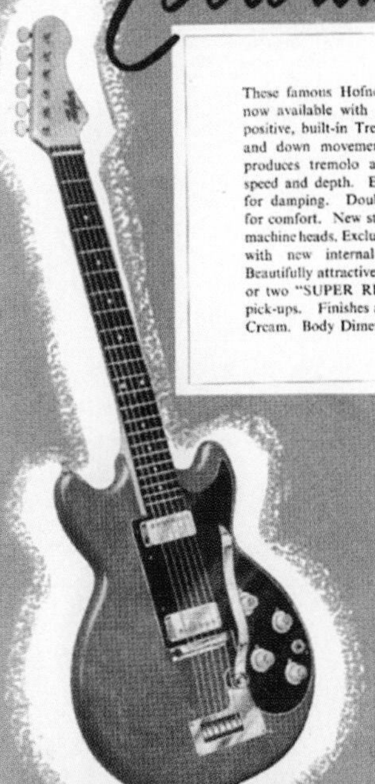

No. 574. Two Pick-up model, with Tremolo **36 gns.**
No. 572. One Pick-up model, with Tremolo **32 gns.**

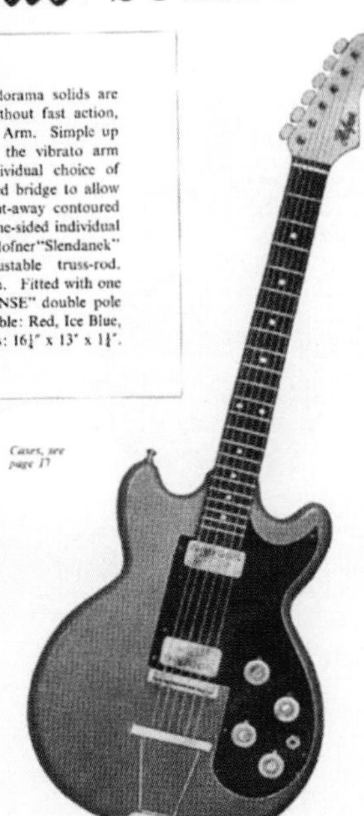

No. 444. Two Pick-up model .. .. **29 gns.**
No. 443. One Pick-up model .. **25 gns.**

NEW Committee

Britain's "top six" guitarists have contributed to the specification of this fine guitar. The Committee Model has a 17¼" top, hand carved from matured straight grained pine. Domed back and sides are veneered in birds eye maple with handsome mother of pearl purfling. Fitted with exclusive Hofner "Slendanek" with new adjustable internal truss rod. Rosewood cambered fingerboard inlaid with mother of pearl on marquetry panels. The magnificent head is inlaid with mother of pearl. Fittings are of a standard which measure up to the guitar workmanship. Screw cog, steel worm, individual dust-proof enclosed machine heads with pearl buttons; fitted with elaborate console tailpiece; new Micromatic Bridge, floating transparent fingerplate.
Body Dimensions : 20¼" x 17¼" x 3".

No. 369. Committee Model, blonde   50 gns.
No. 368. Committee Model, brunette   48 gns.

Cases, see page 17.

13

PRESIDENT

Hofner designers have fixed the width of the lower bout at 16½". The table is hand carved from a block of aged, close grained Bohemian pine. F-holes are bound with white purfling whilst the edges of the table and domed back are purfled with contrasting black and white lines. Maximum vibrations are carried by the **new Micromatic Bridge**. Fitted with exclusive Hofner "Slendanek" with new adjustable internal truss rod. Rosewood fingerboard cambered for fingering comfort. All inlays are genuine mother of pearl. The head is faced with acrylic and gold inlaid, and is fitted with plated and engraved single machines. Best quality lyre style tailpiece.
Body Dimensions : 20¼" x 16½" x 3½".

No. 370
President, blonde
31 gns.

No. 371
President, brunette
29 gns.

Cases, see page 17.

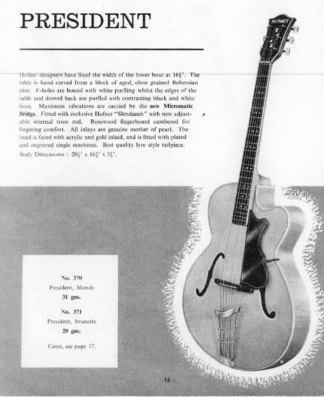

14

SENATOR

The full arched top has new style bracings which give maximum vibrations and contribute to the powerful penetrating tone. The full 16½" body is dimensioned for playing comfort and tonal brilliance. Domed back and top are heavily purfled with contrasting black and white lines. The Senator model is fitted with an adjustable bridge and floating fingerplate in a handsome tortoiseshell finish. Fitted with exclusive Hofner "Slendanek" with new internal adjustable truss rod and rosewood "comfort contour" fingerboard. The head is fitted with screw cog solid barrel individual machines. Best quality nickel-silver fret wire. Compensator tailpiece.
Body Dimensions : 20¼" x 16½" x 3½".

No. 372.
Senator, blonde   19 gns.
No. 373.
Senator, brunette   18 gns.

Cases, see page 17

CONGRESS

Full arched top and back with new style internal bars for greater resonance. Fitted with exclusive Hofner "Slendanek" with new adjustable internal truss rod. Rosewood fingerboard with inlaid mother of pearl position dots and easy action brass frets. Steel screw cog, brass single plate machine heads. Floating fingerplate in rich tortoiseshell finish. Hand-made adjustable bridge. The body has white purfled edge, rich brown colour with sunburst shading and is hand-rubbed to a high lustre finish. The Congress model has an easy action and the tone is very responsive. Compensator tailpiece.
Body Dimensions : 19½" x 15" x 3½".

No. 377. Congress Brunette   15 gns.
Cases, see page 17

15

Hofner SPANISH GUITARS

All Hofner Spanish Guitars have 12th fret to body

FLAMENCO

Full 14" body, wide spaced strings on 2" neck. Close grained pine soundboard with hard laminated sides and back. Spanish-style loop fitting bridge. Long wear steel screw cog, brass worm machines. Hand varnished body. Double purfled rosette. Duro-nylon strings. Well balanced bass and treble for rasiqueado or punteado work.

No. 378. Flamenco   10 gns.

Cases, see page 17

VIENNA

The Vienna model is built to concert specification with 2" neck. Screw cog machine heads. Wide rosewood fingerboard. Carved rosette on Swiss pine body. Flamed sides and back. Loop style rosewood bridge. Discreet brown finish. Nylon strings.
Body Dimensions : 14¼" x 19" x 3½".

No. 376. Vienna   15 gns.

MODEL "222"

Spanish style bridge, fixed fingerplate. Rosette and soundboard edges purfled. Carefully fretted fingerboard with position dots. Good quality screw cog machines, back finish fiddle brown, light gauge wire strings.
Body Dimensions : 13½" x 18" x 3½".

No. 344. Model "222"   7 gns.

16

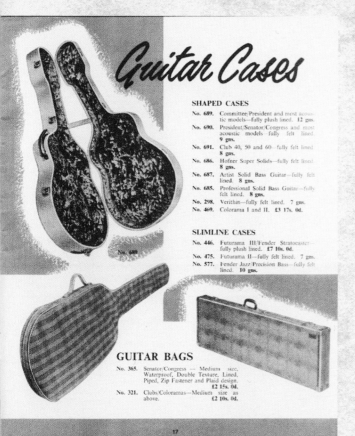

Guitar Cases

No. 689

SHAPED CASES

No. 689. Committee/President and most acoustic models—fully plush lined. **12 gns.**
No. 690. President/Senator/Congress and most acoustic models—fully felt lined. **9 gns.**
No. 691. Club 40, 50 and 60—fully felt lined. **8 gns.**
No. 686. Hofner Super Solids—fully felt lined. **8 gns.**
No. 687. Artist Solid Bass Guitar—fully felt lined. **8 gns.**
No. 685. Professional Solid Bass Guitar—fully felt lined. **8 gns.**
No. 298. Verithin—fully felt lined. 7 gns.
No. 469. Colorama I and II. £3 17s. 0d.

SLIMLINE CASES

No. 446. Futurama III/Fender Stratocaster—fully plush lined. **£7 10s. 0d.**
No. 475. Futurama II—fully felt lined. 7 gns.
No. 577. Fender Jazz/Precision Bass—fully felt lined. **10 gns.**

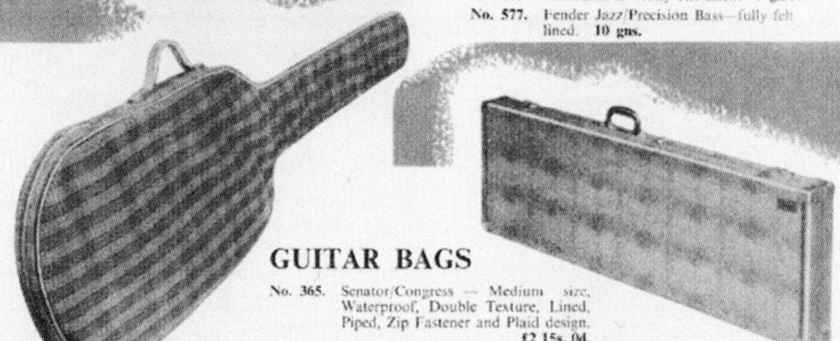

GUITAR BAGS

No. 365. Senator/Congress — Medium size, Waterproof, Double Texture, Lined, Piped, Zip Fastener and Plaid design. **£2 15s. 0d.**
No. 321. Clubs/Coloramas—Medium size as above. **£2 10s. 0d.**

HOFNER

TAPEWOUND STRINGS

These super response friction free strings have been specially designed for the electric guitar. By winding with flat metal tape wire instead of round wire, the strings are super smooth enabling soundless movement over the frets and increasing playing speed.

3033.	First	1/- each
3034.	Second	1/3 ,,
3035.	Third	3/6 ,,
3036.	Fourth	4/- ,,
3037.	Fifth	4/9 ,,
3038.	Sixth	6/- ,,
3039.	Set	£1 0 0 set

HOFNER WIRE WOUND STRINGS

A special light gauge string which has been widely adopted for acoustic and electric work by Frank Deniz, Jack Llewellyn, Roy Plummer and other top-line players.

Prices, each :

285.	First	10d	288.	Fourth	1/6
286.	Second	10d	289.	Fifth	2/0
287.	Third	1/2	290.	Sixth	2/6

206. Set 8/6 set

GIBSON

GUITAR STRINGS

Every Gibson string is wound by hand to ensure finest tone, accuracy of pitch, strength under tension and longer wear.

SONOMATIC ELECTRIC

2092/E332.	First	1/9 each
2093/E333.	Second	1/9 ,,
2094/E335.	Third	3/8 ,,
2095/E336.	Fourth	4/2 ,,
2096/E337.	Fifth	5/6 ,,
2097/E338.	Sixth	6/- ,,
2098/E340.	Set	£1 2 6 set

ELECTRIC SPANISH

2099/E232.	First	1/9 each
3000/E233.	Second	1/9 ,,
3001/E235.	Third	3/4 ,,
3002/E236.	Fourth	3/9 ,,
3003/E237.	Fifth	4/6 ,,
3004/E238.	Sixth	5/- ,,
3005/E240.	Set	19/6 set

HI FI FLAT WOUND

3013/032.	First	2/6 each
3014/033.	Second	2/6 ,,
3015/035.	Third	6/4 ,,
3016/036.	Fourth	7/6 ,,
3017/037.	Fifth	8/4 ,,
3018/038.	Sixth	10/4 ,,
3019/040.	Set	£1 17 0 set

POLISHED COMPOUND BRONZE

3006/932.	First	2/10 each
3007/933.	Second	2/10 ,,
3008/935.	Third	7/6 ,,
3009/936.	Fourth	8/3 ,,
3010/937.	Fifth	9/6 ,,
3011/938.	Sixth	10/3 ,,
3012/940.	Set	£2 1 6 set

ELECTRIC BASS

3020/051.	First	£1 3 9 each	3022/053.	Third	£1 8 0 each
3021/052.	Second	£1 6 9 ,,	3023/054.	Fourth	£1 19 0 ,,

3024/055. Set .. £5 5 0 set

FENDER

GUITAR STRINGS

The many fine qualities of Fender Mastersound Flatwound Strings have won the acclaim of leading players everywhere . . . their superiority will be readily noticed each time you restring with Fender Mastersound Strings.

SET 10

Pure Nickel Wrap—Electric Spanish Guitars.

4080/11E.	First	1/6 each
4080/12B.	Second	1/6 ,,
4080/13G.	Third	2/8 ,,
4080/14D.	Fourth	3/3 ,,
4080/15A.	Fifth	3/3 ,,
4080/16E.	Sixth	3/10 ,,
4080/10S.	Set	15/- set

SET 60

Electric Spanish Guitar—Flat Wound Gold Set.

4082/61E.	First	1/9 each
4082/62B.	Second	2/4 ,,
4082/63G.	Third	4/11 ,,
4082/64D.	Fourth	6/5 ,,
4082/65A.	Fifth	7/7 ,,
4082/66E.	Sixth	9/- ,,
4082/60S.	Set	£1 12 0 set

SET 50

Electric Spanish Guitar and Flat Chrome Wound.

4081/51E.	First	1/9 each
4081/52B.	Second	1/9 ,,
4081/53G.	Third	4/5 ,,
4081/54D.	Fourth	5/3 ,,
4081/55A.	Fifth	5/10 ,,
4081/56E.	Sixth	7/4 ,,
4081/50S.	Set	£1 7 0 set

SET 80

Electric Bass—Flat Wound Chrome.

4083/81G.	First	£1 1 0 each
4083/82D.	Second	£1 4 6 ,,
4083/83A.	Third	£1 8 0 ,,
4083/84E.	Fourth	£1 11 6 ,,
4083/80S.	Set	£5 0 0 set

SELMER

TENSIONED STRINGS

An established range of precision wound all-purpose strings.
Medium gauges laid down after extensive tests amongst a wide cross-section of players.

PLECTRUM 1st, 2nd steel ; 3rd, 4th, 5th, 6th covered.
HAWAIIAN 1st, 2nd, 3rd steel ; 4th, 5th, 6th covered.
NYLON 1st, 2nd, 3rd monofilament ; 4th, 5th, 6th covered.

PLECTRUM

250.	First	6d. each
251.	Second	6d. ,,
252.	Third	10d. ,,
253.	Fourth	11d. ,,
254.	Fifth	1/3 ,,
255.	Sixth	1/6 ,,
256.	Set	5/6 set

ELECTRIC PLECTRUM

264.	First	8d. each
265.	Second	8d. ,,
266.	Third	1/2 ,,
267.	Fourth	1/8 ,,
268.	Fifth	1/9 ,,
269.	Sixth	2/- ,,
270.	Set	7/- set

HAWAIIAN

257.	First	6d. each
258.	Second	6d. ,,
259.	Third	6d. ,,
260.	Fourth	11d. ,,
261.	Fifth	1/3 ,,
262.	Sixth	1/6 ,,
263.	Set	5/- set

ELECTRIC HAWAIIAN

271.	First	6d. each
272.	Second	6d. ,,
273.	Third	6d. ,,
274.	Fourth	1/4 ,,
275.	Fifth	1/9 ,,
276.	Sixth	2/- ,,
277.	Set	6/6 set

SPANISH (Nylon)

244.	First	8d. each
245.	Second	1/- ,,
246.	Third	1/2 ,,
247.	Fourth	1/8 ,,
248.	Fifth	1/9 ,,
249.	Sixth	2/- ,,
250.	Set	8/- set

ELECTRIC GUITAR BASS

323.	First (G)	8/6 each
324.	Second (D)	12/- ,,
325.	Third (A)	15/- ,,
326.	Fourth (E)	21/- ,,
243.	Set	56/- set

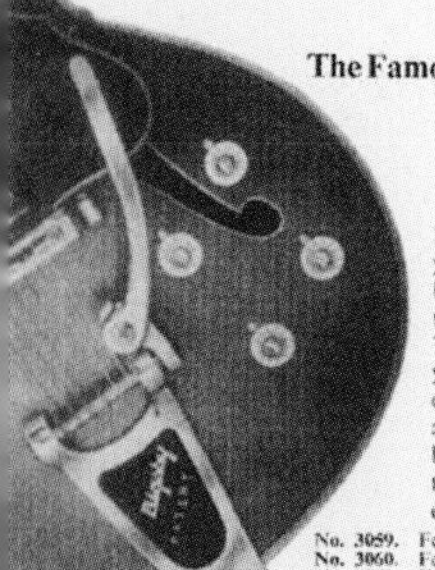

The Famous **Bigsby**

'TRUE VIBRATO' UNIT

Bigsby's unique Tremolo Unit allows you to sharpen or flatten by half a tone by simple up and down movement of the Vibrato Arm. The exclusive Bigsby Tremolo action gives you Tremolo at your individual choice of speed and depth. Supplied complete with "rocker action" bridge which prevents "sawing" by the strings specially designed so that it will not tip. Complete unit easily fitted to any guitar.

No. 3059. For F-hole Guitars.
No. 3060. For Solid Body Guitar with Normal Bridge.
No. 3061. For Solid Body Guitar with Low Bridge.
No. 3092. Without hinge. For Thin Solid Body Guitar.
Price 12 gns. complete.

Also available heavily plated with 24 carat gold 8 gns. extra.

PLECTRUMS

BERT WEEDON

The Bert Weedon Plectrum is identical in shape to the type used by Bert. Both compo and shell models are embossed with a gold name style which serves as a grip.

No. 347. Compo .. 1s. 0d.
No. 348. Real Shell .. 2s. 0d.

GIBSON

No. 3068. Les Paul—Medium.
No. 3078. Les Paul—Flexible.
No. 4087. Ivory White.
No. 4088. Shell.

All 1s. each

ACCESSORIES

The following Hofner accessories as fitted to the various models, are now available.

MACHINE HEADS (3 *on a plate*)

		per pair
510.	Committee, Old Model	£4 2 6
511.	President, Old Model	£2 17 6
512.	Senator/Congress/Vienna, Club 40 and 50	£1 4 6

Single plate type. Specify left or right

		each
507.	Committee	13 0
508.	President, Club 60, Electric Bass Guitar, Verithin	8 9
509.	Senator, Congress, Colorama and Solid Bodies	4 0

PICK GUARDS

514.	Committee	18 6
515.	President/Senator, Club	14 6
516.	Congress	12 6

BRIDGES

687.	Micromatic (*see illus. p. 2*).	£1 10 0
517.	Committee Bridge, Club 40, 50 and 60	15 0
518.	President/Senator/Congress	7 6
520.	Vienna/Flamenco	8 9

TAILPIECES

561.	President Guitar	£2 10 0
522.	Senator/Congress	13 6

De Armond

MODEL 610
Combination Volume and Tone

For the first time—a highly perfected combination of *both* Volume and Tone range. Actuated by nylon gears and racks . . . minimum noise level . . . no lubrication.

Volume increased or decreased by vertical motion. Tone controlled by pivoting foot horizontally . . . left for bass . . . right for treble. Two phone jacks for plug-in from either side.

No. 2054 .. .. 14½ gns.

MODEL 900

More sound . . . less work. Beautiful voicing can be obtained by amplifying the low frequencies with De-Armond's Bass Microphone.

TOPS when plucking, slapping or bowing. No special strings required. No holes to drill—no screws to set. Precision volume control.

No. 2053 .. .. 14½ gns.

MODEL 1000
"Rhythm Chief"

Now . . . a pickup that retains true guitar tones without the stiffness of conventional electrics.

Changes from solo to full rhythm electrically by just a flip of finger. Undistorted power volume. Detachable cable.

No. 2052 .. .. 15 gns.

Guitar Straps

Best quality leather, nylon covered foam cushioned shoulder pad, washable nylon lined. (Assorted colours).

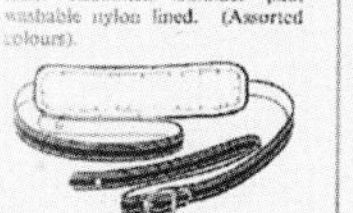

No. 682 .. .. £1 1 0

Selmer 'Polishine'

GUITAR POLISH

Cleans, polishes, preserves, will keep guitars looking new.
Apply a small amount on soft cloth ; rub to a bright lustre.

No. 236
3s. 6d.
Packed 1 doz. to display.

Jiffy Guitar Stand

Here at last is a rigid guitar stand which you can use with confidence. Easy slide assembly with folding pivoted legs. No metal touches guitar as contact points are padded. Heavily plated metal frame folds to 17¼". Weight only 19 ounces.

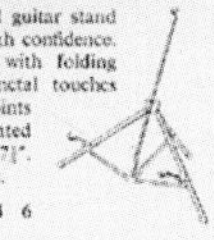

No. 419 .. £1 4 6

NEW HOFNER GUITAR PICK-UPS

POPULAR

Reduction in the price of this *new* pick-up has been effected purely by simplifying the design of the Standard Model No. 352. The sensitivity is unimpaired. The Popular Model comes complete with lead and jack plug.

No. 320 Popular Model £2 3 6

CELLO TYPE

Many top-line guitarists use magnetic pick-ups. Models 352 and 349 have screw-slot adjustable pole pieces for individual string response adjustment. *New* model with integral volume control has improved graduated linear response. Pick-up can be affixed to any cello guitar.

No. 352	Standard Model	£3 2 6
No. 349	With volume control	£4 7 6

ROUND HOLE TYPE

For round sound hole guitars, this *new* model is exactly the same integral design and will give the same high standard of reproduction as the established cello type. The *new* fitting enables the pick-up to be secured on the edge of the sound hole without damage to the soundboard.

No. 345	Standard Model	£3 2 6
No. 346	With volume control	£4 7 6

DE LUXE

This "SUPER RESPONSE" pick-up exclusively fitted to Hofner guitars.

The unique arrangement of the six-pole pieces completely eliminates the overpowering second string tendency found with many pick-ups. This double pole model is a great advance in design and the individual screw adjustments give you correct frequency response on each string, plus higher sensitivity than ever before.

No. 548 .. £6 0 0

SINGLE PICK-UP PICKGUARD UNIT

A *new* self-contained unit for cello guitar. Converts your standard acoustic to a top grade electric model. Easily fitted as the sensitive magnetic pick-up is built into the chrome-plated fingerplate which is fitted with tone and volume controls.

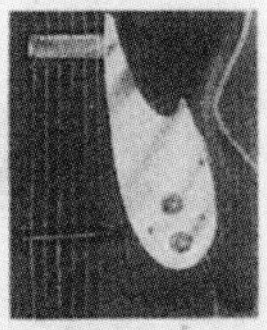

No. 319 .. £4 7 6

TAILPIECE CONTROL PICK-UP

Here at last is the complete conversion set for the player who wishes to use his existing guitar for electric work.
The standard pick-up is connected by a covered cable to a tone and volume control unit which can be fixed to most tailpieces.
Fitted with "rhythm and solo switch." Both units are clear of the soundboard and do not affect the guitar's acoustic properties. The connecting lead is insulated and permanently connected to both units and in consequence **the tailpiece control unit cannot be supplied separately.** Both units heavily plated.

No. 322. Tailpiece Control Unit £6 5 0

DOUBLE PICK-UP PICKGUARD UNIT

This revolutionary *new* pick-up enables two separate heads to be moved to any position between the bridge and fingerboard by simple sliding action. Tonal colours are subsequently infinitely variable, giving complete tonal perfection. A separate magnet for each string on both pick-up heads banishes tuning problems. Control is by dual volume control knob and three "new line" flick switches. With this combination many novel effects are obtainable such as banjo and mandolin tones. The unit is in one piece and is finished in mirror chrome. Easily fitted to any guitar by slotting into the bridge.

No. 506 .. 12 gns.

Printed in England

COMMITTEE
ELECTRIC

Hofner

A committee of Britain's top six guitarists contributed to the specification of this fine instrument which now incorporates an outsize famous classic Hofner head. Fitted with two Hofner high-efficiency bar pick-ups, the guitar has an 18" table and an exclusive Hofner "Slenda-nek" with internal adjustable truss rod, plus ebony fingerboard inlaid with mother-of-pearl on marquetry panels. The magnificent head is inlaid with mother-of-pearl marquetry. Screw cog, steel worm, individual dustproof enclosed machine heads with pearl buttons. Domed back and belly, elaborate console tailpiece. Fitted with Micro-matic Bridge and floating transparent fingerplate. Body Dimensions: 21¼" x 18" x 3¼". (Standard model).

No.5123/06.   Committee, blonde **92 gns.**

No.5123/05.   Committee, brunette **90 gns.**

No.5908.   Plush-lined shaped
case for above .. **£18 10 0**

No.5123/061. Committee, blonde.
Thin model   .. **92 gns.**

No.5123/051. Committee, brunette.
Thin model   .. **90 gns.**

No.5908.   Plush-lined shaped
case for above .. **£18 10 0**

Cases, see page 34

HOFNER BAR PICK-UP
A brilliant new pick-up designed by Hofner, which gives excellent response over the whole tonal range. The bar magnet provides equal balance on all strings and eliminates the overpowering second string sensitivity found in conventional pick-ups.

2

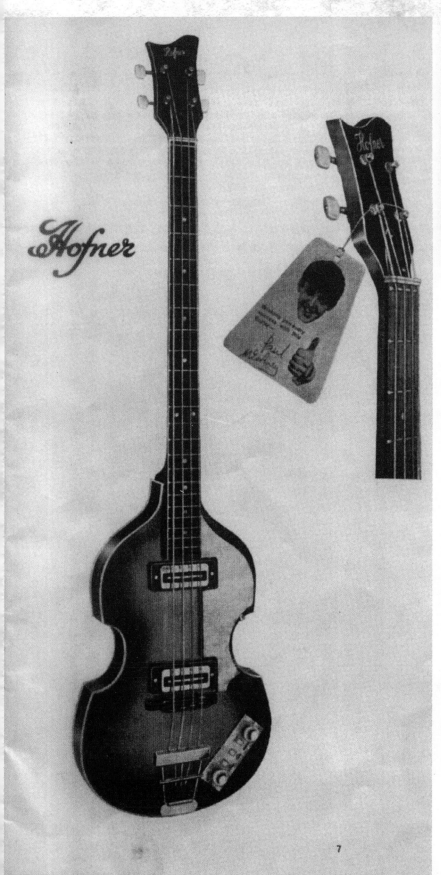

HOFNER
VIOLIN BASS
AND
VIOLIN GUITAR

HOFNER VIOLIN BASS

The world's most famous bass, the Hofner Violin Bass, as used by Beatle Paul McCartney. Fitted with two Hofner high-efficiency bar pick-ups (see page 2), and flick-action switches for instant tone change, this guitar is a favourite with many groups for its powerful, rich tonal quality.

A superb instrument for today's modern players. Attractive brunette sunburst finish.

Body Dimensions: 18″ x 11″ x 2½″.

No. 5150. Violin Bass .. **63 gns.**

No. 5965. Rich felt-lined shaped case for above .. **£13 5 0**

HOFNER VIOLIN GUITAR
Exclusive to Selmer, London
(Not illustrated)

We introduce by public demand the Hofner Violin 6-string Guitar. This unique instrument incorporates all the exciting features that have made Hofner the biggest name in guitars today.

Slim-line neck, easy play action and fingerboard, perfect balance and a flick action switch for instant tone change. Fitted with two Hofner high-efficiency bar pick-ups (see page 2). Also there are three controls—one for volume, and two for tone.

An attractive sunburst finish adds lustre to this unique instrument.

Body Dimensions: 18″ x 11″ x 2⅛″.

No. 5136. Violin Guitar .. **68 gns.**

No. 5936. Rich felt-lined shaped case for above .. **£14 0 0**

Cases, see page 34

7

Acknowledgments

We would like to thank the following people, without whose help – either wittingly or unwittingly given – this book would have been more difficult to compile.

Philip Armstrong
Rob Armstrong
Tony Bacon
Christian Benker
Brian Bennett
Bill Brent
Garry Burnett
Steve Clarke
Neil Cope
James Cumpsty
Mark Cunningham
Paul Day
Terry day, Dennis Hill & Alan Goodes
Rob Fodder
Hilary Giltrap
Dave Halton
John Hammell
Dave Hodson – (Mac-1 Music, Loughborough)
Eric Haydock (Rhythm House Music)
Pauline Heath
Tom James
Gerard Kelly
Electric Ladyland
Lastolite
Nova Darkroom Equipment
Tom Orellana (Music Inn, Nottingham)
Bill Puplett
Eddie Reed
Steve Rowley
Sax Mad Simon (Music Project, Liverpool)
Norbert Schnepel & Helmuth Lemme
Mark Steadman
Debbie Taylor

Naturally, we apologise for any omissions.